S0-CMP-964

VIOLENCE IN THE HOLY LAND

VIOLENCE IN THE HOLY LAND

Witnessing the Conflict in the Middle East

Edited
by
Robert Wolf

Decorations by Bonnie Koloc

FREE RIVER PRESS
Lansing, Iowa

Copyright © 2004 by Free River Press. All rights reserved. Except for brief excerpts for reviews, no part of this publication may be reproduced or transmitted in any form or by any means, electronic or mechanical, including internet, photocopy, compact disc, recording, or any information storage or retrieval system, without permission in writing from the publisher. First edition. ISBN: 1-878781-25-1

1. Israeli-Palestinian Conflict 2. Israel. 3. Palestine. 4. Middle East

FREE RIVER PRESS
Lansing, Iowa 52151

www.freeriverpress.org

CONTENTS

EPILOGUE

INTRODUCTION

Violence in the Holy Land is a record of the ongoing violence in Israel and Palestine, written by Jews and Arabs. Most have had firsthand acquaintance with the conflict. Some were born in the Middle East, others were born in the United States and have traveled to Israel and Palestine or made their homes there. They have recorded their experiences with passion and clarity. When I think of their stories, I see an elderly Palestinian, forced years ago from his village by Israeli soldiers into a refugee camp, playing his radio constantly, hoping to hear the announcement of the Palestinian right of return. I picture an Israeli journalist, a young woman, standing in a street littered with body parts. Or an American Palestinian at a checkpoint, confronted by the arrogance of a young Israeli soldier. Or a Jewish family in America worrying over the fate of a son serving in the Israeli Defense Forces, searching Palestinian homes.

All have something pertinent to say not only about the violence in Israel and Palestine, but by implication about human nature itself. Over the last several centuries the world has been in the process of transforming itself into a Theater of Violence. The number and ferocity of conflicts seem to intensify by the year. The situation in Israel and Palestine is particularly painful. Horrors no less acute have been perpetrated in Africa, Northern Ireland, Kosovo, Bosnia, and elsewhere, but the unrelenting nature of this conflict, begun well before the creation of the State of Israel in 1948, makes this the most publicized theater of violence. Retaliation and retribution follow each act of provocation. Israeli-Palestinian history has become an automaton grinding out actions and reactions ad infinitum with all the predictability of a machine. The conflict between Israelis and Palestinians is mirrored in the ancient Greek myth of murder and counter-murder within the Tantalid family, fashioned by Aeschylus into a trilogy of plays, *The Oresteia*, covering four generations of murder and revenge. At the conclusion of the story the Furies, who avenge the murder of blood relatives, hound Orestes, the last in

1

the line of murderers, until he seeks sanctuary in the temple of Athena in Athens. The goddess assembles Athens' first jury to determine his guilt or innocence. When their verdict is deadlocked, Athena breaks it, declaring Orestes innocent. Aeschylus' point is obvious: reason must rule over the furious dictates of murderous instincts; law must replace blood vengeance. But note that it took a goddess, standing proxy for transcendent revelation, to break the cycle of vengeance.

The historical roots of Jews and Arabs mirrors the Greek myth of the Tantalids, for both peoples trace their descent from Abraham. For the Jewish people the ancestral line proceeds from Abraham and his wife Sarah to Isaac; for the Arabs it is traced from Abraham by the Egyptian woman Hagar through their son Ishmael. Just as the murders in the Tantalid family were the murder of cousin by cousin, so too it has been for Jew and Arab. But where did their conflict begin? Where does any historical event begin? If we attempt to come closer to the truth by examining smaller and smaller units of activity, we find that no matter how small the unit or event we examine, we find that it, too, has a cause, which means we cannot we locate the beginning of any event. History is a continuous movement of happenings, which is one reason why there can never be an end to accusations by either party in such a dispute.

Listening to the demands of each side in the conflict brings us back to two of its proximate causes: to the founding of the State of Israel and, according to U.N. figures, the displacement of well over 800,000 Palestinians. We know, of course, that both events have roots further back in time. The founding of Israel marks the fulfillment of an ancient dream, which, like the Jewish diaspora, is announced in Deuteronomy. There we read that God told the ancient Hebrews, "If you fail to observe faithfully all the terms of this Teaching that are written in this book, to reverence this honored and awesome Name, the LORD your God, the LORD will . . . . scatter you among all the peoples from one end of the earth to the other . . . Yet even among those nations you shall find no peace, nor shall your foot find a place to rest . . . ."

Introduction

The diaspora came in 70 AD, when Jews living in the Roman province of Palestine revolted. The insurrection was put down, the second Temple was destroyed, and the Jews were exiled, eventually making their way to every corner of the world. By 1880 approximately 500,00 Arabs and 24,000 Jews resided in Palestine. Following the First World War, the Sykes-Picot Treaty divided Turkish-held Arab lands into British and French-administered regions. Palestine was divided approximately in half, into TransJordan and into present day Palestine and Israel, administered by Britain. The 1922 British census of Palestine revealed a population 87.6 percent Arab and 11 percent Jewish. The 1931 British census counted a population of slightly over 1 million, with 84 percent Arab and 16 percent Jewish. By 1937, Jews counted for 28.24 percent of the population. The present conflict arose out of the Arab fear that a continual stream of Jews emigrating to Palestine would eventually overwhelm them. As the number of immigrants grew, sporadic rioting and killings erupted throughout the early twentieth century. Nazi persecution and the murder of 6 million Jews in the Holocaust brought even more immigrants. Finally, a two-state solution was proposed as early as 1947 by the United Nations and was accepted by the Zionists but rejected by Palestinians on two grounds: first, that they were offered a smaller portion; second, that it was their land that was being occupied.

By a variety of means—conquest of war, purchase, illegal seizures—Israel has greatly expanded its territory since the nation's founding on May 15, 1948, but the result has always been the same for Palestinians—dispossession and displacement. The Israeli government's actions have created a large Israeli peace movement, but despite this, a minority of Israelis, consisting of right wing and religious parties, continue to wield a disproportionately large share of power and use it to create numerous settlements in what is left of Palestine—the West Bank and Gaza—thus creating a need for army protection and infrastructure, including roads. All of this costs money, which is drained from projects in Israel itself. On top of this, ultra-orthodox Jews are exempt from an otherwise universal military conscription.

As of this writing, the ultra-orthodox are resented by many fellow Israelis for getting a "free ride" and for provoking Palestinians with the creation of new settlements. These fundamentalist Jews, many of them American, embrace Messianic Zionism, an extreme form of Zionism which seeks to recreate the ancient boundaries of Greater Israel, enlarging the land to what it was in the days of self-rule under King David and later, the Hassmoneans.

For their part, Muslim fundamentalists are opposed to Israel's existence. Through repeated suicide bombings, Hamas and Islamic Jihad seek to destroy Israel and replace it with an Islamic Palestinian state. The defeat of the armies of Arab states in the Six-Day War fueled the fundamentalist movement, as did the overthrow of the U.S.-backed Shah of Iran by Shiite Muslims. What Muslim fundamentalists seek to create are theocracies in which Islam provides the answer to all social and political questions. By their very nature, Jewish and Muslim fundamentalists are irreconcilably opposed to each other, all the more so because they seek to control the same land.

The situation is further aggravated by the influence of American Christian fundamentalists who are a powerful force in American politics. Because they believe that the Second Coming of Christ is imminent, and because it supposedly will coincide with the conversion of the Jews and the fulfillment of ultra-orthodox territorial ambitions, Christian fundamentalists provide Israel with unqualified support.

But what are the boundaries of the ancient land? The most explicit statement occurs in Genesis 15:18, where God tells Abraham, "Unto thy seed have I given this land, from the river of Egypt unto the great river, the river Euphrates." The land between the Euphrates and the river of Egypt—the Nile—encompasses portions of Syria, Iraq, Saudi Arabia and Egypt itself. While some Zionists and Christian fundamentalists dream of bringing this land once again under Jewish rule, "thy seed" refers to both Arabs and Jews, the descendants of Ishmael as well as Isaac.

4

Introduction

◆◆◆

The Israelis are caught in a trap. Every act of violence on their part calls forth a deadly Palestinian response, and vice versa, to the extent that Israel has become, in effect, a vast prison. Where will the next suicide bomber strike? Will Israel be attacked by a deadly gas or virus? What does one do? Wear a gas mask? Avoid crowds, restaurants, night spots, cafes, certain bus routes? Leave the country? Join peace demonstrations? Cast another vote for Likud? Even now a wall between the West Bank and Israel, like the one between Israel and Gaza, is under construction, absorbing land beyond Israel's 1967 boundaries.

As for the over 3 million Palestinians living in U.N. supplied refugee camps in nine surrounding Arab countries, those of us who live in American prosperity can only imagine what it is like living in crude cinder-block houses, on dirt streets with open sewage channels, without work, in host countries that do not want us. Can we imagine the plight of another 3 million Palestinians living in refugee camps and towns in occupied territory, where the Israeli army strikes swiftly and murderously to retaliate against the families of suicide bombers? Or in villages where Jewish settlers armed with automatic rifles prevent Palestinians from harvesting their olive crops?

The Oslo Accords and the Wye River Agreements laid the basis for the gradual transfer of land and governance from Israel to the Palestinian Authority and the establishment of a Palestinian state. But the extremists on both sides have thus far made a peaceful resolution impossible, and U.N. resolutions have done little or nothing. Only the withdrawal of U.S. financial aid, which keeps Israel afloat, would force concessions from Israeli leadership, but this is hardly a possibility. The present U.S. administration, which alone has the leverage to bring about serious negotiations, sat by for two years before working an agreement with other countries on the so-called Road Map, which in itself will do nothing. The current leaders of Israel and the Palestinian Authority, Sharon and Arafat, are bitter antagonists and their respective administrations are charged with corruption.

(One member of Sharon's cabinet has even floated the idea that killing Arafat would be a possible solution to the problem!) What is manifestly clear is that announcements, declarations, treaties and resolutions have accomplished little or nothing. Force has accomplished nothing except to inflame both sides. Only a profound change of heart will accomplish anything. What else could possibly bring about a cessation of suicide bombings and new settlements, the two absolute preconditions for negotiation? Since the conflict is prolonged by the extremists, the future in great part lies with them.

But the problem of reconciliation extends beyond the extremists to the moderates. It is not uncommon to hear a moderate Jew or Arab, even those who seek dialogue, claim that you cannot trust the other side. Each accuses the other of being tribal; each accuses the other of betrayal. Family and communal histories are unrolled and examples cited. True or not, fact or fiction, they are enormous burdens; they lead to assumptions that make peace an ever receding possibility. On the Israeli side there is a fear even among some intelligent Jews that every Arab seeks the destruction of Israel. "Everyone knows that," a Jewish friend assured me. Both sides fear that the other seeks its extermination.

Various myths, perhaps grown from solitary incidents, persist. ("Jews abduct and murder Arab children." "In my grandfather's day, Arabs cut fingers and other body parts off of Jewish children.") Murders from previous generations are cited to prove that friendships between the sides are feigned. In such a climate, where fear spawns deep distrustfulness and hatred, there is an ever greater need for men and women of goodwill, the moderates from both sides, to gather and hear each other's fears and misconceptions.

As of this writing, the Geneva Accord, born of informal dialogues in non-governmental sessions, remains the only hope for peace. Developed by Palestinians and Israelis, including former Palestinian Information Minister Yaser Abed Rabbo and former Israeli Justice Minister Yossi Beilin, the plan meets many of the demands and needs of both sides. But Ariel Sharon has reportedly called it "the greatest historical mistake since Oslo" while former Prime MInister Ehud Barak characterized it as "delusional."

Whether such dialogue will ever spark an inner transformation, the words of the Koran stand as witness for the one precondition for peace: "Verily never will God change the conditions of a people until they change what is in themselves." (Sura Al-Ra'd, 13:11) This truth is repeated in every authentic tradition. Hillel the Talmudic sage, when asked by a Persian to teach him the entire Torah while he stood on one foot, repeated the words of Jesus: "Love thy neighbor as thyself," adding, "All the rest is commentary."

◆◆◆

This book grew out of three weeks of writing workshops intended primarily for Israelis and Palestinians, but open to anyone with direct experience in the ongoing conflict in Israel and the Occupied Territories. The workshops were made possible primarily through a grant from The Puffin Foundation in Teaneck, New Jersey, which had sponsored several Free River Press community writing workshops in Teaneck in the winter/spring of 2002. One of the writers in those workshops, Nitza Horner, came from a family that had lived in Palestine and what is now Israel for seven generations. When I asked the writers to introduce themselves, Nitza explained that she was a sculptor and had taken up her art as a way of retaining her sanity after her brother died in 1974, while on duty with the Israeli army. She was fourteen at the time and in school when a teacher told her he was wounded and warned her not to cry. The teacher accompanied the family to the hospital, and there repeatedly signaled Nitza to repress her tears, even after she learned of her brother's death. Nitza later told the story in small part to a few friends, and in detail to a boyfriend who slapped her when she cried, after which she thought that she was purged of the pain. I asked Nitza to write about the experience, using all the sounds, smells, and sights at the hospital she could recall, to put us in her place. The editing process pushed her, she said, "towards painting the piece"—using imagery, and into universalizing the experience. With the writing an emotional dam burst, and while not freed of its burden, she made a step toward confronting the experience.

From our homes half a continent apart, we began talking about a collaboration. For years I had wanted to run workshops in Northern Ireland, between Catholics and Protestants. But with Nitza's story in mind, and the increasing violence in Israel and Palestine, I thought it was important that we do a book on the Palestinian-Israeli conflict. Nitza agreed, and I approached the Puffin Foundation, which seized on the idea immediately. With the help of the Puffin Cultural Forum's program director, Tim Blunk, we began approaching individuals and institutions for possible writers. In June 2002, the Puffin Foundation held an open house with a presentation for interested area residents. About half a dozen of the attendees, including one Palestinian man, returned for the workshops that began several weeks later. For seventeen days in July, at the Puffin Foundation and at The Riverside Church in Manhattan, I ran workshops for about fifteen individuals.

◆◆◆

The workshop process is orally oriented. We begin by reading aloud stories developed in other Free River Press workshops to let participants know that you don't have to have college training to write effectively. We comment on what makes the story work—its imagery, phrasing, and so on—and then proceed to tell our own stories, which is the heart of the process. Since most groups are composed of people with similar backgrounds (they live in the same town or are engaged in the same occupation) one person's stories spark another's memory. They often know the same people and share recollections. The story Jones tells may prompt Smith to decide to change his topic. Through these means, and by the fact that they ask each other questions about their stories—things they want to know more about—the narratives are fleshed out. I ask them to include dialogue to develop character and action, and imagery to help put us in the scene.

***

Although in almost every piece, implicitly or explicitly, the authors make their perspectives on the conflict clear, these writings are stories, not editorials, illustrating individual but common experiences. Storytelling and a willingness to listen to the other's narrative are the two preconditions for dialogue.

For several years, American Jews and Palestinians have been meeting in dialogue groups across the country. Contributor Marcia Kannry is one of the mainstays of the dialogue movement. Having experienced great personal loss in Israel, she returned to the United States, wanting to find people from both sides to whom she could talk. In the process she discovered dialogue and eventually established The Dialogue Project in New York, which she has expanded to groups in Manhattan, Brooklyn, and New Jersey.

Like Marcia's dialogue sessions, the point of this book is to have people from the other side listen; for if they cannot make peace in the Middle East, individuals from both sides can, at least, make a separate peace across the table. They will not, as Dan Malater and other contributors write, allow themselves to be dehumanized. For all, honest dialogue means being open to the others' pain; it implies listening, not filtering. Nitza, for example, wanted others to have the healing experience she had had, to "put people together and compare each one's broken limbs" and create "a way for people to understand how easy it is to be provoked into extreme behavior."

For the former Israelis during the first week of the workshop, discussion and argument seemed the end in itself. They were very good at dialogue, noisy and passionate, sometimes amazingly adroit. At one point Nitza and Allon Pratt, an Israeli refugee who teaches at the Jewish Theological Seminary, took to role playing. Allon assumed the part of a Palestinian and Nitza the part of a Jew. Having grown up and lived most of their lives with this conflict, they knew the points the other would make, and therefore knew what their own response should be. Their argument was enormously subtle with point and counterpoint, boom, boom, boom without pause for reflection, a bravura performance surpassing any professional improvisation I had ever seen. Early into their dialogue I looked for a tape recorder on the table, assuming for some reason that we had one running. But there was none, and I was instantly deflated, sure that if they tried to recreate their argument that it would lack spontaneity and life.

The issue of dialogue is raised repeatedly in the book, most insistently in the essays of Ofra Dimant and Marcia Kannry. Ofra, who emigrated here from Israel, makes a passionate plea for the other side to tell its stories. Her plea is the perfect compliment to Marcia's story, which outlines the preconditions for dialogue. Together, these two gave me an inkling for the structure of the book. Allon Pratt's fairy tale, describing the friendships between four generations of a Jewish family with its Arab neighbors, is a dream of peace and an ideal prologue, establishing the goal of dialogue. And so, in imitation of dialogue, the book begins with Allon's fairy tale, then Ofra's plea, followed by a Palestinian story, then an Israeli story, back and forth, giving multiple perspectives. In some cases, where two stories from the same side were similar or otherwise related, I placed them side by side. Marcia's story and explanation of the process of dialogue closes the book. The experiences that unite either side are summarized in her image of Israel as the young Jew with a rifle slung over his or her shoulder, standing on a prostrate Palestinian and saying, "Tell me I'm a victim," while the Palestinian says, "Stop making me a victim."

◆◆◆

When I returned home from the East Coast to begin the editing, I had few completed manuscripts. Most stories were in first or second draft. My job over the next three months was to stay on top of the writers until they delivered completed works. We sent drafts back and forth by e-mail, and the writers always had the option of rejecting my edits, which in most cases were light.

Up until the final workshop, few Arabs had participated, and I began fearing that we would never have a book. Fortunately one of Tim Blunk's contacts, Maher Abdul Qatar, past president of the Palestinian-American Congress, arranged for five Palestinians to attend the final Sunday, when the Pratts were also there. Four of the five Palestinians—Mae Ramadan, Ramsey and Nader Abdallah, and Ghassan Shabaneh—wrote drafts that day which they completed sometime later. But even with their work we hadn't enough Palestinian stories, and so seventeen-year-old Mae Ramadan contacted other possible writers. She and her sister Mannal telephoned a cousin in Gaza, who dictated a story over the phone. In addition, Mae wrote Ramzy Baroud, editor of *The Palestine Chronicle*, about the project. Not only did Ramzy contribute a story, "Dying on the Side of the Palestinians," but he solicited articles from three West Bank residents—Sam Bahour, Amer Abdelhadi, and Ali Samoudi. These last four contributions filled important voids in the picture. Thanks are due Mr. Baroud for translating Ali Samoudi's lengthy account of the Israeli incursion into Jenin and to *Tikkun:A Bimonthy Jewish Quarterly of Politics, Culture & Society*, for permission to reprint Sam Bahour's story, "Perfecting the Violence of Curfew." (*Tikkun*'s website: Tikkun.org) Thanks also to Loree Rackstraw for forwarding e-mails written by Germana Nijim from Palestine. The workshops were made possible through the generosity of Roger Isaacs and, most especially, Perry and Gladys Rosenstein of the Puffin Foundation, whose financial support and belief in dialogue made the workshops possible. Thanks to the Foundation for Middle East Peace and its president, retired ambassador Philip C. Wilcox, Jr. for funding the publication of this book, as well as to all those subscribers who purchased advance copies.

VIOLENCE IN THE HOLY LAND

PROLOGUE

■ *Allon Pratt*

Allon Pratt, a seventh generation Sabra (Israeli born), was a kibbutz member in the Negev Desert for twenty years. As a teacher and father of five, Allon returned to the university to earn another degree in Arabic language and culture as part of his effort to communicate and bridge gaps between Arabs and Jews. Since 1998 he has lived in self-imposed exile in the USA.

A FAIRY TALE

More than one hundred years ago, my grandfather, Sabba Gad, grew up in the old city of Jerusalem. His best friend was Amin al-Husseini. They were very naughty as kids. One night they played a trick on the whole town: they met halfway between the Jewish quarter and the Muslim quarter and together they switched all the signs in town. The midwife became the cobbler, the butcher turned into the Mohel. You can imagine the confusion and anger that filled the town the next morning when a very pregnant woman walked into the cobbler's shop and a baby ready for circumcision was brought to the butcher's store... The two kids were scared and ran away to hide in a safe haven. My Sabba Gad hid behind the curtain of the ark in his neighborhood synagogue, and Amin, his friend, ran to hide in the mosque of his quarter.

It so happened that the rabbi was my grandfather's father, and the kaddi in the mosque was Amin's father. Both fathers figured out that their kids had collaborated in that mischief and took their sons, respectively, towards each other. They met halfway between the Jewish and Muslim quarters and had a "serious talk." The kids were not punished but rather they promised never to do to others what they did not want done to themselves. As they were looking up to their fathers and making their promise, the rabbi and the kaddi with their beards and shining eyes and noble looks, seemed to them to look like the

12

prophet Elijah, the Messiah, and their mutual promise became an unspoken covenant, that was enhanced by the sound of flutes and drums coming from the alleys of the old city of Jerusalem.

Years later, my mother grew up in the budding small coastal town of Haifa. Her best friend was Jamilla, the daughter of their Arab neighbors. Together they went swimming in the sea, or wandering through the market, or hiking in the ravines and slopes of Mount Carmel. Once on a vacation day, they went via the market to get supplies for a day of hiking. They bought nuts and raisins and almonds and figs and carobs and set forth to the mountain. They reached the peak of Mount Carmel, where there is a statue of the prophet Elijah. Jamilla whispered into my mom's ear that a tradition in her family says that if you squint your eyes in front of the statue, and look carefully into the eyes of Elijah, they start to shine and move and smile at you. And that would be the perfect moment to make a wish. Both Jamilla and my mom did just that: they squinted at Elijah, and his eyes moved and smiled back, and they whispered a silent covenant which was reaffirmed by the sounds of music coming from the market of Haifa.

And again, years later, growing up in Israel, I had a Bar-Mitzvah project to do in school: "My Neighbors." I teamed with a Druze boy from a nearby village. Wallid was a very hospitable, smart, and fun-filled kid. As a matter of fact, our families became very friendly. They would visit us at home, bringing fruit from their orchard, and we would visit them in their village, bringing vegetables from our patch. We would have sleepovers at each other's homes and visit each other's classrooms. Once, while picnicking near Wallid's village, we wandered off into the woods, and arrived at the foot of the statue of Elijah. I quickly whispered into Wallid's ear that a tradition in my family says that if you squint and look carefully into Elijah's eyes, they start to shine and move and smile back at you, and that would be the perfect moment to make a wish. Both of us did just that: we squinted at Elijah. His eyes moved and smiled back at us; as a matter of fact, it seemed as if his whole body was beginning to come to life and move. And the faint sounds of flutes and drums from the fields of Wallid's village reinforced a silent covenant.

Guess what? Years later, my daughter Gahl is a typical kibbutz girl, growing up out in nature in the dunes of the Negev desert. Her friend is Aziza, a Bedouin girl from a neighboring tribe. They pay each other visits for Haflas at Aziza's tent, or holiday celebrations in our kibbutz. Once, when on an outing to explore ants and insects and gerbils and cacti in bloom, a sudden sandstorm started to twirl around the girls. Somewhere between Gahl's kibbutz and Aziza's tent they huddled, eyes closed, the storm whirling around them. When the twister rolled away, they both confessed to having seen Elijah the prophet go up to the heavens with his chariots of fire. And it was a moment of awe, and a mute covenant with you-know-what music witnessing it.

POINTS AND COUNTERPOINTS

■ *Ofra Dimant*

Ofra Dimant immigrated to the U.S. from Israeli in the late 1980s with her husband and three sons. She teaches school in Teaneck, New Jersey.

A MOTHER'S THOUGHT

My God says, "No child should lie under a stone, for the sake of guarding a stone."

The Arab-Israeli conflict started for me in 1956 at age nine, when Dad went off to fight in the Sinai Campaign, and I sat daily on the front steps waiting for him, until he returned home.

Eleven years later the Six Day War engulfed the region, and I served in the army as a medic. My job was to examine the Kalandia airport in East Jerusalem, and I saw the dead left in the streets, and I had to examine sanitary conditions in the city.

There was a sense of exaltation at the news of taking over the Old City, at the idea of conquering the Kotel, the Western Wall, our holiest site. It all returned to us, it was ours, according to Israeli propaganda.

Approximately a year later, Professor Yesha'ayahu Leibowitz declared that "The conquest is a calamity for Israel. Euphoria will soon dissolve, and then the real problems will start."

As time went by, I got married and had three sons. I remember the 1973 Yom Kippur War. My dad consoled me by saying not to worry, because surely Ran, Eyal, and Yaron would not have to serve in the army.

Along came 1990. Ran left for the army. Although we had been living in the U.S. for a while, it had not occurred to any of us that there could be an alternative, such as not serving in the army. The army was a sacred concept, above any other consideration or dispute. This was the value system at home: an education towards fulfilling Zionism and never deserting.

Ran served in the Occupied Territories. In spite of being worried sick here in the States over anything that was happening over there, scared of every phone ringing—or not ringing—in case something bad happened to Ran, it still seemed obvious, beyond question, that Israel must be in the Occupied Territories in order to protect the safety of its citizens.

Ran finished his military service in 1993, and Eyal enlisted a year later, and I repeated the same pattern of anguish and fear.

In 1996 Rabin started the process of the peace talks. Peace is here, just around the corner!

Economically, politically, and socially all is wonderful, and then Rabin's murder, definitely the low-point of Israel's existence. Everything is disintegrating. No more understanding, no trust on either side. The media is blowing things out of proportion, and the human landscape is polarizing into extreme fanaticism. Leadership gave permission to an ever-increasing extremist behavior on the part of the army and in the public's attitudes.

Conquest is mother of all evil. I believe that as long as we do not pull out of the Occupied Territories unconditionally, there will never be a possibility of co-existence.

In 2000 my husband and I went with friends for a vacation in Dahab, Egypt. Our driver was a Bedouin Arab. He would take us sight-seeing during the day, and swimming or eating out during the evenings. One night he invited us for tea in his home. It was a stone house with a sand floor. We lounged on carpets and cushions in his hosting area. His wife and children sat quietly around us, and while we were drinking tea together he said to us: "I want peace and quiet. I want to earn the money that will enable my children to study, that will enable me to purchase a television for my home and food for the kids. I want to make a living respectably and with dignity. We have no interest in a leadership that tries to convince us that you Jews are only interested in taking away our lands."

People make peace. The leaders will find any reason to continue the conquest only because of the fear of losing the helm. And in the meantime, civilians and soldiers continue to die.

The extremists on both sides run the show nowadays. Religious fanaticism in both people causes the leadership to hesitate in making a rational decision. Each side blames the other for not considering the other's needs.

May I as a mother believe that calm will one day prevail? Can anyone explain to me why terror does not cease? Barak said once, "Had I been a Palestinian, I would have become a terrorist." Does this make mothers feel more secure? Do Israeli mothers feel calmer when their sons are in the territories? Sons who are eighteen years old, carrying weapons. Isn't the norm worldwide for kids at this age to be studying, traveling and enjoying life without worries?

◆◆◆

When will the Arab-Israeli conflict end? Where will it take us? How does one stop the vicious cycle of terror, reoccupation, expansion of settlements, terror, occupation, etcetera, ad infinitum?

Who will be the strong person to halt this horrid perpetuum mobile by simply saying, "No more"? Will that person rise from within the ranks of the Palestinians, establish a democratic rule and eradicate terror gangs? Will Israel find a leader strong enough to say, "Thus far, and no further," one who will abolish the settlements and draw a borderline between the two states, and resolve the conflict?

How can anyone justify the army's behavior when a boy is murdered while getting off a bus thinking soldiers are guarding him on the road, or when a mother is critically injured and the fetus is murdered inside her? Does Israel have the right or the need to protect its citizens and do all it can to prevent such atrocities from happening? And is it indeed only terror, as the Palestinians claim, that can prevent the settlements, the abominations at the checkpoints, the hunger and the degradations?

Will we ever solve problems by blaming each other?

I never had the opportunity to sit down and talk with somebody from the other side. I need the situation explained from the opposite perspective—the thoughts, the feelings, and the behavior patterns of the people from the other side of the barricade. Perhaps if a true dialogue were to develop, an honest and responsible one, between the people, if the real truth were to emerge, perhaps it would be possible to eradicate both parties' behaviors.

Is it at all possible to educate a whole people to change character and thought processes, to see the world through the eyes of the other side, so that positive behavior will emerge on both sides? Who has the courage to undertake this education? Who is prepared to do that and to leave behind frustrations and suspicions, and instead to focus on the light at the end of the tunnel? What must happen before we wake up?

Dying on the Side of the Palestinians

■ *Ramzy Baroud*

Ramzy Baroud is a Palestinian-American journalist and the editor of Palestine Chronicle, *a leading Palestinian on-line publication. His columns have been published in the* Guardian, Le Monde, Christian Science Monitor, Seattle Post Intelligencer, Jordan Times, Daily Star, Arabia.com, Arab News, Jerusalem Post, *and elsewhere. He was born and raised in a refugee camp in the Gaza Strip and currently resides with his wife Suzanne and two daughters, Zarefah and Iman, in Seattle, Washington.*

DYING ON THE SIDE OF PALESTINIANS

"Ramzy, I must admit it, it's so hard being a Palestinian these days." That's how a friend of mine, a dedicated individual who is spending her days and years advocating justice for the Palestinian people, ended a distressing message to me a few months back. I recall her words often, and as often I recall my grandfather who died in a refugee camp's mud home, away from his village and land.

My grandpa believed that being a Palestinian was a blessing. "You cannot be entrusted to defend a more virtuous cause than the cause of Palestine, unless Allah has blessed you greatly," he once told me.

I often wondered what kept the old man going. He lost his home and the pride of his life, his land, and was forced at gunpoint to haul his family away and leave the village of Beit Daras where they once lived happily. He spent the rest of his life, getting old and tired in a refugee camp, for many years in a tent, then in a mud house subsidized by the United Nations. He died there, next to a transistor radio.

Grandpa's radio was once green, yet its color faded to white somehow. It was battered, and covered with duct tape, just enough to keep it whole. The old man cared little for the look of the radio. All that mattered was that the radio managed to broadcast the news. The "Voice of London" (in Arabic), the "Middle East Radio" or the "Voice of the Arabs" were constantly on. At night he tucked the radio beside him and went to bed, to start his next morning with the latest news.

He fancied that one of these days the radio would declare that Palestinian refugees were allowed to go back home. He carried that fantasy until he died, at the age of ninety-five, decades after he was forced out of Palestine.

We would see Grandpa walking toward the radio briskly from the kitchen, or waking up abruptly from an afternoon nap, fervently asking, while pointing at the radio, "Did they just say something about refugees?"

"No, Grandpa, they haven't," one of us would reply with a juvenile smile. He would return back to his chore, carrying the weight of many years, and his unending hope.

But Grandpa died a few years before the start of the Palestinian uprising of 1987. He was too old to walk, to argue with Grandma for not feeding the chickens on time, or to converse with an ailing neighbor. But never too old to hold his little radio, lovingly, with a final desperate hope that the long awaited news segment about his return to his village would be declared.

When Grandpa gasped his last breath, all of his friends and family stood by, muttering verses from the Quran as many tears were shed that day. I, too, stood near to him, frightened of confronting my first experience with death. He made it easy on me, as he had a smile on his face, and near him was a radio with the volume lowered but never muted.

The year of his death was a year that many older refugees also passed away. They were buried in a graveyard surrounded by the graves of younger refugees, mostly martyrs who fell throughout the years.

I wish I could have managed to keep Grandpa's old radio. I haven't. But when I left my refugee camp, I did manage to smuggle many memories, his undying hope, and his pride of being a Palestinian.

Very often, and now more than ever, I recall the words of my friend about how difficult it is being a Palestinian these days. I recall it with every Palestinian child killed or home demolished, with every speech that President Bush makes outlining his visionless vision of the Middle East; I recalled it when a

Can We Find One Another?

Brussels' court denied Palestinians the right to try Ariel Sharon for his massacres in Lebanon; I recalled it when a Dutch officer held me for a long time, delaying the entire flight while investigating me for the mere fact that I was born in Gaza; I recall it when I read the *New York Times* or the *Washington Post*; I recall it when my father talks to me on the phone just to tell me that the Israelis are bombing his neighborhood; I recall it not every day, but every hour.

But I also recall my grandpa's words: "You cannot be entrusted to defend a more virtuous cause than the cause of Palestine, unless Allah has blessed you greatly."

I often wondered why old, dispossessed, and ailing Grandpa died in a mud house with a smile on his face. We will all die one day, rich and poor, citizens and stateless, Palestinians or Israelis, presidents or refugees. It's that final and decisive moment, when Grandpa gasped his last breath that counts. He lived a hard life, a refugee, with his dearest possession, a battered transistor radio. But he died a Palestinian who never compromised on his rights. He died proud, with a smile, leaving us with nothing but a transistor and an abundance of hope.

Grandpa never returned to his village of Beit Daras, but I know that one day my children will.

■ *Helen Pincus*

Helen Weiss Pincus is the associate editor of The Jewish Standard *and* The Jewish Community News. *She studied nutrition at Hebrew University in Israel and worked as a research assistant at the Weizmann Institute in Israel in structural chemistry and has been a faculty member at The New School in New York City and at The Ma'ayanot Yeshiva High School in Teaneck. Her freelance articles have appeared in* The Record, *the* New York Times, Lifetime, Big Apple Parent, ParentGuide, *and* The Parent Paper.

CAN WE FIND ONE ANOTHER?

I am looking for that time again when it all connects. Where the differences are not as important as that vast warm comfort which holds us all together.

The young Arab man we had been waiting for arrived, wearing jeans and a denim jacket; his dark curly hair shone with random golden flecks. He was a teacher and was eager to meet Jews who came to Israel. He, like my friends and me, was interested in forming alliances from which we could all grow.

"I want you to meet my father," he said and he led us, a group of foreign scientists and students, out to an adjacent field where a small stooped man, filthy with sweat and dirt, pushed a crude ancient plow through the rich soil. Perfect furrows formed in the old man's slow moving wake. The furrows were short but there were many and the sun was harsh. We walked through the scruffy weeds at the field's edge and approached the man through an unplowed section, where the soil was still packed hard.

The young man lifted his father's hand, and kissed it reverentially. Dirt had formed demarcation lines in the wrinkles and scars.

"This is my father," the young man said with such pride that we all wanted the privilege of kissing his father's hand. An almost toothless smile formed on the older man's face, and he muttered some Arabic words of welcome. His few teeth were yellowed. His smile was dazzling. How like my father he was on some essential level. Yet I have not been able to pass this reverence on to my basically decent children.

This Israeli Arab farmer and my European Jewish father, both somewhat beaten down by physical labor but with their dignity intact, would have enjoyed sharing a cup of tea or coffee or fresh squeezed orange juice. They knew that their children would treat them with respect. And they would have agreed that killing is bad.

This is where we need to go back to. What we lost. Where we begin to learn. Arabs and Jews must return to this starting point and take pride in this heritage.

22

Can We Find One Another?

◆◆◆

I can't stand the pain anymore. Wounded. Dead. Each person is a world and the loss robs us all. Complex people worlds are being shattered into air and we breathe them in and are not transformed. We don't know if they loved yellow or blue. We don't know if they were awful, aggressive drivers, or if they could tell a joke the right way. So many places in Israel should be filled with sweet laughter and absurdity. Those places are being shattered.

The entrance to Jerusalem, when you come on the Sha'ar HaGai Road, past the destroyed vehicles of the 1948 war which are left as memorials, is guarded by a day glo orange lion. Jerusalem's symbol is a lion; this one and others scattered throughout the city, each decorated by artists, were part of the Jerusalem Day festivities celebrating the day Jerusalem was reunited after the Six Day War.

The day glo lion should be funny, the object of scornful or joyful derision. And the crazy intersection of Yafo and King George Streets, that too should be funny, with crosswalks in five different directions as if designed by a theoretical physicist who had studied too much kabbalah. It should be funny but the rebuilt Sbarro's Pizzeria is right there and so are the souls of the people who died when a homicidal maniac wearing a belt filled with evil destroyed that place. And it's not funny. Some things can't be repaired. I just want everyone to be back again, intact with nothing missing and no poison soaked nuts or bolts embedded in our souls or brains or legs. I want us to be together harvesting hyssop and cooking chicken covered in tehina, breathing in the pungent delicious food aromas which heal all pain. How I miss being able to make fun of the Israelis. I remember complaining about how different we Americans are from them. Wasn't that fun? Wasn't that the best time? How filled with hope we all were. We can't complain now. If the Arabs were really smart they would leave us alone. We Jews could destroy Israel very well without any help, thank you. Or maybe not.

23

Maybe then we Arabs and Jews, secular and religious, socialists and capitalists, could work it out and figure together how to stop the traffic accidents, cure cancer, and create schools and economies that work. We need to connect on common ground with common people. Isn't there enough common ground for us to share?

♦♦♦

When I was a child sitting on our front porch in New Jersey, shaded by chestnut trees, everything seemed to be possible. Why didn't it translate into the wider world? Was it the chestnut trees? Couldn't the olive trees provide the same message? Was it something about my parents, arriving middle-aged in a foreign country, pursued by the hounds of hell, with one small child and one on the way? Were they magic that they could create a reality that had room for so many people with different beliefs to exist in the same indefinable ether?

♦♦♦

Bruriah was afraid to come. Her family was Yemenite. Her parents had suffered under Arab rule for years and had no love for them.

Convincing Bruriah was never easy. She was stubborn, worldly-wise and just knew things. But I was older and American and I could be persuasive when I was determined.

Finally she agreed to come with me to have supper with Tamim's family in the Arab village. Tamim was a student I had met at the agriculture school where I was studying nutrition.

He met us at the bus stop and showed us around the village. Everyone looked at us with mostly benevolent curiosity. Tamim's parents welcomed us to a table filled with delicacies.

"It tastes like home," Bruriah said.

To me she whispered, "Tamim's mother looks like my mother."

Can We Find One Another?

◆◆◆

Maybe it wasn't true. There was no sign in the hallway, no white sign with stark black letters announcing his death. We had heard he was lost in battle, somewhere in Sinai, and then we heard he had died. But it was all rumors and then there was no sign. In Israel they always post signs when someone dies.

So we walked up the marble steps to Tzvika and Ruthy's apartment to be reassured because there was no sign that said the polite blue-eyed strikingly handsome lieutenant, who was their younger son, was dead.

But when the door opened the pain hit and their faces, even had they not been sitting on those low Shiva stools, said he was gone.

◆◆◆

Why couldn't they just leave that little tiny sliver of Israel, filled with broken Jews who had survived the Holocaust? How dangerous was this U.N. mandated state that would shelter the remnants of my people? Why did the Arab countries start the war that created the refugee problem? Why did they leave the refugees in those miserable camps while squandering millions of dollars of humanitarian aid on weapons?

It is a fantasy that Jews and Arabs lived in peace before the State of Israel was founded; there were only brief moments. In 1929, Hebron, where Arabs and Jews had lived peacefully as neighbors, turned into a city of terror and murder. By the time the massacres ended, sixty-seven Jews were dead. And again in 1939, Jews were massacred in Hebron. You can't speak about peace to people who are unwilling to examine their own faults, their own complicity. The rabbi's question that rankled the young Muslim man from Paterson is legitimate: "Do you think Palestinians should kill Jews? Do you? You didn't answer the question. We mourn for your dead. Why do you celebrate our deaths?"

Jews and Arabs can co-exist, I hope. Israel is far from

perfect but it is the only democracy in the Middle East. It is the only country in that region that allows citizens of all religions to worship freely, openly. Israel respects the diverse houses of worship within its boundaries, and Israel has Arabs in the Knesset. The other Arab states are terrified of what might arise out of Palestinians and Jews working together to create an oasis of power, sanity, and peace.

What the Egyptian-born Arafat has done to the Palestinian people (while amassing a significant personal fortune with money that was to be used to build an infrastructure to provide his people with education and comfort, and keeping his high-life-style non-Muslim wife, Suha, and their daughter in luxury digs in Paris) is a crime. The Israelis are the only people in the Middle East who are not encouraging the Palestinians to turn themselves into weapons. I know there are Palestinian mothers who love their children as much as we love ours. Can we find one another?

■ *Ramsey Abdallah*

Ramsey Abdallah was born in the United States; his family is originally from Jerusalem Palestine. He is a graduate of New Jersey Institute of Technology and currently running the regional operations for a northeast New Jersey real estate firm. Ramsey is a founding member of the Middle Eastern Policy

Political Action Committee, which is built on the true vision of what the Middle East will be one day.

TASHEEN DARWEESH

In the summer of 1982 I was three years old. Some would say, "What does a three year old know?" or "What can a person remember from his life at three?" One thing comes to mind immediately is the name "Tahseen Darweesh." He was my cousin. That summer he and my older brothers had bonded to become a cohesive unit of soul mates. Eighteen years old, he stood at 6'1" and had the strength of three men. He worked late and returned late to our village of Beit Douqqo.

At that time the war in Lebanon was the heated topic of debate, and stirred mixed feelings in Palestinians. We remember an attempt that was made on the life of an Israeli official. Everyone blamed *Fatah*. Who was *Fatah*? Everyone was *Fatah*.

One day, as they had been doing their military rounds through the villages, the Israeli police picked Tahseen up as he was coming home from work. Tahseen went missing for three days before he was brought back home, dead. He looked like nothing of what we remembered. He was destroyed. His once beautiful aura and appeal were no longer. His eyes were gauged out; his arms were broken in five places. There were cigarette burns on his neck, arms, and back. His neck was blown up three times its normal size, which was found to be caused by a pair of denim jeans that had been forced down his throat. His wrists were cut to the bone with the wire ties that had been used to restrain him. It looked as though he had been trying to escape from them. His legs were tenderized like veal from the butts of rifles. The Israelis did not return the body to Tahseen's house; they left it in the middle of the street. My brothers, who were his best friends, had to go and carry his body to his grave. To this day my brothers have nightmares about what they saw. Years have gone by since his death, yet those memories remain. From that moment I became very worried for what the fate of others would be. These were acts of hate and malice; these weren't in the defense of anything.

■ *Nader Abdallah*

Nader Abdallah lives in West Orange, New Jersey. He is a gradute of Rutger's University and is a first year medical student at Midwestern University. Nader was born in New York, the youngest of eight children. His family is originally from Jerusalem Palestine.

MOHAMMED AHMED DAOUD

It was a hot summer day without even a slight breeze to dry the sweat off my brow. I sat there crying over a grave filled with dust that embodied my one and only true friend. His name was Mohammed Ahmed Daoud; he was killed by Israeli soldiers. I remember that day too well. It was December 17, 1998. I had just got back my midterm from my A.P. chemistry class and was overjoyed with the results. "Now, I can go to Florida and relax in the sun," I said to my friend as we were driving home. The trip was a present for my mom's birthday. It was also an excuse to leave New Jersey for the winter break. Senioritis, a disease that infects all seniors in the high school, was setting in and I wanted to take the trip after my midterms were over.

As we drove up to the house, my friend noticed that there were too many cars in the driveway. I got scared. This usually meant that either something happened to one of our family members in the States or overseas. I got out of the car, walked to the door, and was met by my brother-in-law taking out the trash. I greeted him, and saw by the look on his face that something was wrong. I walked into the house and saw everyone sitting in absolute silence. I began to prepare myself to hear that my grandmother had passed away. I stood in the middle of the room and began asking, "What's wrong. What happened?" I looked at the faces and saw that my mother's was bright red and moist with tears. I turned to her for a response, but she kept on with the rest of them, saying, "Nothing's wrong." I was getting ticked off that no one was telling me what was going on.

My father looked at me and said, "They killed your friend!" Confused, I took a step back, thinking that he meant my friend who had just dropped me off. My mother saw the terror and confusion in my face and began to elaborate, as she cried, that Mohammed Ahmed was killed in Ramallah during a demonstration. I was in a state of shock. I dropped the books I was carrying. I flung my glasses to the wall, cracking them in half. I ran out into the streets like a madman, yelling and cursing, hitting my head and slapping my face. I immediately wanted vengeance. I didn't care in which form it came, just as long as I could make that killer's family feel what I was feeling. I was so enraged that I found myself in front of a wooden shack in a neighbor's backyard and hitting it, imagining I was beating down the terrorist who killed my cousin. I fell to the ground and began wailing like a little baby; at that point my parents found me and brought me back to the house.

In my religion there is a period of forty days in which the family mourns over their lost one. One of the rules is not to shower for a week, or something to that effect. I broke it as soon as I got home. I jumped in the shower to try and gather my thoughts. I convinced myself that the corpse that was found had my cousin's "ha-weeyah," or identification card lying near it, that he was just hiding until the army left the area and everything would be fine. I cheered up and felt almost like a genius for being the first to realize that it was all a case of switched identities, or something to that effect. I decided to cheer up my mom with the news. She began to cry and say, "*Inshallah*," which means, "God willing." As far as I was concerned, I was being the most rational of the group. My denial didn't last long. When my father heard me defending my case, he became enraged. He thought I was making fun of the situation. He yelled, "His brothers identified the body. There is no way it couldn't be him!"

I fell back into my dark pool of sorrow, dismayed by the failure of my reasoning. I became depressed. I began having nightmares. At times I would see him happy and laughing, when all of the sudden blood would pour from his mouth and he would collapse. Behind him would be an Israeli soldier with the gun, carrying a big smile.

I spent most nights in my bedroom speaking to apparitions of Mohammed Ahmed. I would speak to the apparitions and they would reply. I would stay up until I fell asleep, when I would feel him shake my hair and say to me, "See you tomorrow, kid."

I began gathering as many clippings of the incident as I possibly could.

I lost my cousin, who was more than a brother or a friend. We were inseparable. I began thinking that if there were a guarantee that I would meet up with him after death, that I would commit suicide. Through the help of my friends (including an Israeli teacher and her family) and most importantly my family, I came to terms with his death. I went back to see his grave.

And here I am, sitting in this horrible sun, wondering if he can hear me. "God, I wish some breeze would come by here. Mohammed Ahmed, it's hot as hell." Before I knew it, the sweet smell of flowers filled the air and a beautiful breeze took away the heat. It's him, looking out for me, just as he did when he was alive. "Rest in peace, *habibee* (my love)."

■ *Heidi Gleit*

Heidi J. Gleit was born in Philadelphia in 1972. She moved to Israel in 1994 and worked as a journalist at The Jerusalem Post *and as a foreign press liaison at the Hebrew University of Jerusalem. She currently lives in Tel Aviv.*

HOPING FOR PEACE WHILE LIVING WITH TERROR

The names of the websites shocked me: "Wake Up or Die," "Jews for Allah," "Radio Islam." While I knew that the articles I had written during my six years at *The Jerusalem Post* had circulated widely—my father alone had e-mailed my articles to pretty much the entire Philadelphia Jewish community—I had never expected to see them on websites like these. The articles I had written about social issues in Israel, with the naïve hope that they would move the efforts to improve life in Israel forward a step or two, were being used as evidence to promote hatred of Israelis and Jews on dozens of anti-semitic and anti-Israel websites.

As I sat in front of the computer at my parents' home in Philadelphia shortly after leaving Israel in August 2002, I felt betrayed and disappointed that my efforts to do something positive had been cynically manipulated again. I still believe that the articles I wrote about social problems in Israel added an important component to the Israeli debates on women's rights, alleviating poverty, lowering crime, and dealing with the dilemma posed by tens of thousands of foreign workers, but I wonder if they were premature. Maybe all those taxi drivers and politicians were right when they told me that Israel had to focus all of its resources on solving the conflict with its Arab neighbors, a problem which threatened the life of all Israelis, and only after that was solved would it be able to address the other issues, problems which lower the quality of life of some Israelis. I am not quite convinced, especially since it does not seem right to neglect these issues indefinitely as the Arab-Israeli conflict drags on and on with no resolution in sight.

31

For as long as I can remember, Judaism and Israel have played a central role in my life. Perhaps it was the Jewish day school in Philadelphia that I attended. Or perhaps it was the specialness of the occasional trips my grandmother and I would make to spend a Jewish holiday with my uncle and his family in their small synagogue in the heart of the Orthodox community in Baltimore. Or maybe it was simply that every Friday night my parents invited friends, family and visitors from Israel to join us for a Shabbat dinner at which my siblings and I would compete to show off who had memorized more words of the prayers and who knew more of the various rituals.

Whatever it was, by the time I reached high school, I was strongly committed to Judaism and knew that I wanted to live in Israel. The influences that led me to want to be a reporter were equally strong. And so, in addition to working on my high school paper, I was the editor of the newsletter of the local Zionist youth group. Then, after school, my friends and I would go to the local public library to research the forefathers of Zionism—Zeev Jabotinsky, A.D. Gordon, Rav Kook, Ahad Ha'am—so we could teach the other members of our youth movement about them. We were enchanted by the romantic idealism of their lives and writings.

I had moved to Israel and become an Israeli citizen shortly after I finished studying journalism at the University of Pennsylvania. I did not renounce my U.S. citizenship and appreciated the values that America stands for and the opportunities it provides, but I was attracted strongly to Israel. Unlike many Americans who move to Israel, I never ruled out the option of returning to live in the U.S., even though I think it is unlikely that I will ultimately make the U.S. my home again.

I arrived in Israel in the summer of 1994, several days after Yasser Arafat's triumphant arrival in Gaza. He had come to build a Palestinian state; I had come to build a life for myself and begin my career as a reporter in the Jewish state. At the time, enthusiasm for the peace process was high, though the peace process was, as it had been from the start, highly controversial. All of the Israelis I encountered liked the concept of making peace with the Arabs, but many questioned whether a man with a penchant for violence and a contempt for democracy was capable of leading the fractionalized, fractious Arab world to coexist peacefully with Jews and to accept the concept of a sovereign Jewish state. The continual attacks in which Arab terrorists murdered and maimed children and other innocent Israeli civilians going about their daily lives led many to question whether the Arab peoples were ready to make peace. The stories of chaos and corruption emanating from the nascent Palestinian state did not inspire much confidence either.

Skeptical yet hoping to be pleasantly surprised, I set out to learn about my non-Jewish neighbors after I had acclimated a bit to life in Israel. Once I could speak Hebrew fluently, I began to study Arabic, registering for a class at the YMCA along with a handful of journalists and housewives. Pleased with my new ability to say, "Hi. I am a journalist. Do you speak English?" in Arabic, I decided it was time to actually meet some native Arabic speakers. I joined a group of Israelis who spent one morning a week teaching Hebrew and English to Palestinian schoolchildren at a school in the village of El Khadar.

The school was a fifteen-minute drive and a world away from my south Jerusalem apartment. Initially I had been wary of driving there alone in my new car with its bright yellow Israeli license plate. El Khadar was a poor village with few new cars on its unpaved roads, especially Israeli ones. Its residents had been active in the 1987 Intifada, stoning Israeli soldiers and sheltering and supporting anti-Israel terrorists. Now that the peace process was underway, things seemed to have changed. I took the highway out of Jerusalem, drove through the tunnel built recently to protect Israeli commuters from Arab terrorists' stones and bullets, slowed down to pass the army checkpoint, and finally turned onto the small road leading into El Khadar. Residents leaned out of their windows to wave to me as my car bumped over the narrow, rocky paths that led to the school.

Children from Bethlehem and the Dehaishe refugee camp joined children from the village each morning to study at the private school that had been established to promote democratic values. They were eager to learn English and Hebrew and even more eager to learn about us, just was we were to learn about them. We tutored them one-on-one and in small groups using photocopies from English and Hebrew grammar books that one of the volunteers brought as guides. As the only school operating under the auspices of the Palestinian Authority that taught Hebrew and had Israeli teachers, the school did not have a budget to spend on Hebrew textbooks, or many other things, and was frequently harassed by the authorities. Still, the principal welcomed us warmly, teaching us Arabic over the lunch he prepared for us himself each week. The pupils' parents were equally gracious, inviting us to visit them in their small, sparsely furnished homes. Hampered by our inability to speak one another's language fluently, we did not speak about politics but simply questioned one another about our families and the types of foods we liked to eat. In the end, one simple message was conveyed: there are real people on the other side of the Arab-Israeli conflict and some of them are warm and generous and not evil or violent.

One of my good friends from Philadelphia gave me another window into Arab culture in the summer of 1998. A graduate of the same Zionist youth movement as I, she was one of the token Jews on a summer program in Ramallah for American law students. Together we wandered through the streets of Ramallah, aware of our otherness and thrilling in the foreignness of this city so different from and similar to our home, Jewish Jerusalem. We bought *falafel* (deep fried chickpea patties) and *kenafe* (sticky, sweet cheese pastries), went to hear American Jewish immigrants play jazz to Palestinians, Israelis, and Europeans at a nightclub, checked our e-mail at the local internet café and hitchhiked back to her dorm. Along with the rest of her group, we went to a bar to watch the Iran-U.S. world cup game, scared to cheer for either side. We felt that the steps we gingerly took were way beyond those of trendsetters—we were sure that one day we would be able to tell our Jewish-Israeli grandchildren how we had taken those steps that they take for granted because we were among the first pioneers privileged to enjoy the fruits of peace. Perhaps they would even look at us in disbelief as we would tell them how passionately painful our arguments with the Arab-Americans in my friend's group had been because they had refused to acknowledge that the Jewish people had any connection whatsoever to the Land of Israel. Skeptical as my friend and I were of the troubled peace process, we never imagined that barely two years later it would have evaporated to a point where two men would be brutally beaten and tortured to death by the bare hands of Ramallah residents on those same streets simply because they were Jews.

My personal exploration of Palestinian and Israeli-Arab culture was interrupted soon after that summer when my editors at *The Jerusalem Post* asked me to move from Jerusalem to Tel Aviv to be the paper's Tel Aviv area correspondent. Thrilled with the opportunity, I threw myself into my new job working day and night to acquaint myself with the city of Tel Aviv-Jaffa and the surrounding areas. My personal exploration turned into a professional hunt to learn more about my new home and share the interesting parts with the paper's readers. Being *The Post*'s only full-time correspondent in the area meant I had the freedom to write about everyone and go everywhere: from the ceremony for the final status negotiation between the Israelis and Palestinians at the Erez checkpoint at the entrance to Gaza to the remains of a Tel Aviv brothel in which four women had burnt to death after a mentally ill religious fanatic had firebombed it.

I also soon found I was in a unique and somewhat discomfiting position. As an American trained reporter writing for a newspaper with an international readership, I did not fit in well with the Israeli press corps in Tel Aviv. My Hebrew was fluent, but I spoke it with a strong American accent. My clothing and mannerisms identified me as an American even before I opened my mouth. Since I had not grown up there, I did not have the personal connections they had. And my editors were interested in different stories than theirs since we had a different readership.

I did not fit in with the international press corps, either. Unlike many of the foreign correspondents, I felt that I was a part of Israeli society: I had lived in Israel for several years and had obtained Israeli citizenship and worked for an Israeli newspaper that was distributed abroad. To me, the Israelis were not "them," but "us." As professional journalists, many of them had built a wall around themselves, as I had, to separate themselves from the events they covered so that they could cover them impartially. But after work, as we relaxed together and let down our guard a bit, the scorn many of my friends and colleagues displayed toward Israel pained me.

I found myself gravitating more toward the Israeli press corps, finding that I had more in common with them. Or perhaps I simply spent more time with them reporting on stories that were of more interest to Israelis—we sat together on the tile floors in the halls of the Tel Aviv courthouse for countless hours waiting for hearings to start, met on dark corners in south Tel Aviv late at night to survey the scene of a murder and exchanged glances as we listened skeptically to the mayor at press conferences announcing yet another plan to improve the city.

The Intifada that began in the fall of 2000 changed that. Suddenly all of us, Israeli and foreign press, were on alert all the time for the same thing: the next major terror attack or riot. The years I had spent working at *The Post* in Jerusalem had prepared me for this, as I had slowly been eased into covering terror attacks and disasters: coming in to be an extra hand in the newsroom during crises; taking telephone reports from reporters about the chaos and panic at the scene and weaving that together with updates from the police, army, and Prime Minister's Office; going to the hospital to interview the distraught victims and their families; or to the scene to write a supplementary report describing the shattered glass, bloodstained pavements and charred remains of storefronts. The time I had spent covering crime and politics also helped: I knew the politicians and the policemen; I had learned the etiquette of disaster scenes; I had built a wall between myself and what was happening so that it could not touch me.

Other reporters had a less gentle entry into covering terror attacks. One of my Israeli friends simply went into shock and burst into tears upon arriving at the scene of the first terror attack she was sent to cover. Luckily, a more seasoned reporter from her paper was there as well to slap her across the face, pulling her out of her shock, and then calmly directing her to get to work. Covering terror attacks quickly became routine for her, for me, and for most other journalists in Israel. We rushed to the scene and did our work there, along with policemen and soldiers, ambulance drivers and doctors, politicians and protesters, municipal clean-up crews and religious men from the burial societies who would scour the scenes for bloody pieces of human bodies to bury along with the rest of the corpse.

I guess most stories really were connected to the terror attacks and the halted peace process. I went from the funeral of an Ethiopian-born soldier in a small Israeli town to the mourning tents that families of two suicide bombers had set up for their "martyred" relatives in an Israeli-Arab village. Despite the vastly different circumstances of their deaths and lives, the same adjectives were used to describe the three dead young men: "generous," "caring," "family-oriented." Yet one had been cut down by terrorists as he defended the beloved homeland of his ancestors, while the other two, though their families denied it, had intentionally killed themselves and innocent bystanders by setting off bombs.

I felt more sympathy for the Palestinian laborers I met in the yard of the Ramle Police Station in the early hours of the sweltering day they were arrested for illegally residing in Israel. Desperate to feed their growing families, they had walked miles and miles, carefully avoiding Israeli security, to sneak into the Tel Aviv area, where they could work as construction workers, movers, and manual laborers. Once upon a time, over 100,000 Palestinians made the commute from the disputed territories to pre-1967 Israel. It was a short, simple commute—a half-hour taxi ride from Ramallah to Jerusalem, a ten-minute drive from Kalkilya to Kfar Saba—such a simple commute that terrorists could easily traverse it. Dozens of terrorists and would-be terrorists disguised as laborers made this simple trip, carrying explosives in their lunch bags instead of food, and went on to

slaughter hundreds of Israelis. Frustrated Israeli security offi-
cials finally responded by limiting the number of residents of
the territories who could enter Israel and finally by barring all
those who did not have special permits. Since the Palestinian
Authority had made almost no progress in creating jobs in the
territories, tens of thousands of honest laborers were left with
the choice of sneaking into Israel to work or losing face by staying at home and accepting charity. The terrorists had put all of
us in a no-win situation, the laborers agreed. Either Palestinian
children live in poverty or Israeli children get murdered.

"The children need food, so I come here. What else can I
do?" one man told me. "No," he does not remember how many
times he has been detained. "No," he does not have anything
against the police or Israel, he emphasized as the men around
him nodded in agreement. "I just wish there were a more stable
way to earn a living."

Human-rights activists condemned Israel for prevent-
ing the Palestinian laborers from exercising their right to earn a
living. But what about the right of my family, friends, and neighbors to put their children on a bus in the morning without having to wonder if the children will make it home alive? Human-
rights activists also condemned Israel for imposing collective
punishment on the good Palestinians along with the terrorists,
for considering the Palestinians as a single stereotyped entity,
and not as individuals.

None of the Israelis I know did that—we all know and
interact with Palestinians and view them as individuals. We recognized the differences between individuals, but were very
aware of the difficulty of differentiating between them and were
not willing to risk the lives of our children to try to differentiate.
Too many children already had been slaughtered and crippled
by fashionably dressed teenaged girls from rural Palestinian villages, by Muslim fundamentalists dressed in the garb of religious Jews, and by clean shaven Gaza youths clothed in stolen
army uniforms. The terrorists went to such lengths to disguise
themselves— smuggling explosives into Israel by hiding them
under the gurneys of ill, elderly Palestinians on their way to

Israeli hospitals in Red Cross ambulances—that we simply felt there was no other choice.

Though terror attacks had become more and more common in Jerusalem, I moved back there to work in the media department at the Hebrew University of Jerusalem in March 2002. Both Jerusalem and I had changed significantly during the three and a half years I had spent in Tel Aviv. The point was brought home to me a few months later when, crossing the street in front of my apartment building one morning on my way to work, I heard the loud boom of a terrorist blowing up a bus making its way through my neighborhood.

No longer a reporter, I responded like a normal Israeli and mentally ran through the list of friends and relatives who could have been injured and then started calling their cellular phones. The list had become shorter over the past few years and especially over the past few months. Most of my American friends had left Jerusalem for the U.S., dispirited by the depressing economic reality of life in Israel, the deteriorating political and security situation, and the simple difficulty of day-to-day life there. They had grown tired of and frustrated with living under siege in Jerusalem, strategically planning each expedition to the supermarket and wondering if they would make it home alive.

We barely ever thought about going to restaurants and bars, venturing out rarely even to places that we felt were secure—cafes far off the beaten track that had barred windows, security guards, and locked doors. We all longed for our barefoot picnics in the park, at which we feasted on fresh vegetables we had bought in the open market and prepared in our tiny kitchens. The long walks through the Old City of Jerusalem, along with visits to all of the other places that made Jerusalem unique and enchanting, had long since been ruled out as too dangerous.

There also were no more expensive parties at exclusive restaurants to celebrate one another's new jobs and promotions. Those that were lucky enough to have jobs worked long hours for low pay, while hundreds of laid-off high-tech workers desperately searched for work and signed in weekly at the dole office. Volunteering at the school in El Khadar was no longer an option. It was not safe to travel on the highway to the village, which had been identified as a Hamas haven, and the school had closed down after the principal died of a heart attack. It seemed that every week another person I knew was returning to the U.S. and the bulletin boards were full of posters declaring: "Moving Sale; Everything Must Go."

Another fatal terror attack on campus near my office made the changes even clearer than before. Swamped with requests for information from the media and the general public, I barely had time to send my parents a brief e-mail saying that I had not been injured when the bomb planted in one of the cafeterias exploded at lunch time, killing and wounding Israeli Jews, Israeli Arabs, and foreigners. I was frustrated by criticism that the university was not handling the terror attack well—would an American or British university have done better? And why should an institution whose mission is to build knowledge and tolerance be prepared to handle a terror attack anyway? Like my colleagues at the Hebrew University, I was shocked that terrorists would strike at an institution that had been and still is one of the loudest advocates of peace and coexistence.

Five of the nine fatalities had been Americans. Their lives had been so similar to mine. Ben Blutsein had grown up in Pennsylvania and gone to the same summer camp as I. Dina Carter had fallen in love with Jerusalem and settled there. She had become so Israeli that it took us awhile to realize that this gentle, dedicated university employee was the fifth American victim. A call from a social worker in California confirmed that Marla Bennett's parents were now suffering just as my parents had suffered when my brother Jonathan suddenly died in an accident a few years ago. The details of the Israeli victims' lives were just as familiar. I had lived in the neighborhoods they were born and raised in, wandered through the same streets they had.

None of those streets or neighborhoods were the same anymore. The charm and beauty of Israel were difficult to see beneath the grime and blood of terrorism. Feeling close to the breaking point, I decided it was time for an extended vacation in the United States to rest and build up the strength to return and help prevent the beauty of Israel from disappearing under the hatred of fanatics.

■ *Germana Nijim*

A native of Italy, Germana came to the United States in 1958. She was first introduced to the Middle East in 1966, where she spent one year divided between Beirut and the Jerusalem/Ramallah area. She has returned to the Middle East a number of times since. In 1978 she was appointed Director of International Services at the University of Northern Iowa in Cedar Falls, Iowa and served in that position until early retirement in December 2000. Germana was married to Basheer Nijim, Professor and Head of the Geography Department at the University of Northern Iowa for nineteen years. The Nijim family is from Nazareth, but Basheer grew up in Jerusalem. In 2002-3, Germana trained with Christian Peacemaker Teams (CPT). The goal of CPT is to reduce violence in conflict areas, to document cases of human and civil rights abuses, to work for justice, and to support the oppressed.

THE MAKING OF A SUICIDE BOMBER

Wednesday, May 14, 2003

Hamed (not his real name) is thirteen. He lives in the very fertile Beqa'a Valley, a half hour drive from Hebron. He has three older sisters. He is the only boy—at thirteen neither a child, nor a man.

His land is coveted by Jewish settlers, and his house is marked for demolition by the Israeli government. Soldiers beat on the door of the house one, two, three times per night on the pretext of having to search for weapons. The whole family suffers from sleep deprivation, fear, and anxiety.

Settlers come after dark and throw stones at the house. Most of the windows have been shattered. Seeds are dug out of the earth and scattered. Vines and young olive trees are uprooted.

Hamed is often confined to the house because his parents fear for his safety. His oldest sister was studying at the University of Hebron. Now its doors are welded shut. The second sister was attending the Hebron Polytechnic, but that institution has also been shut down. The third sister, fifteen years old, is not planning to go on with her studies. What is the use? she says, looking at her sisters.

A few months ago, Hamed's parents, wanting to give him something he could call his own and make him happy, gave him a puppy. No thirteen year old can resist a puppy, and Hamed fell in love with the little creature.

One evening Hamed called and called for his puppy, but he never came home. In the morning he found the little body on his front door riddled with bullet holes.

Hamed went to his room, wailing, screaming, weeping, repeating a phrase over and over and beating his head against the wall. What was he saying? "I want to be a suicide bomber!" His mother had to restrain him from severely injuring himself. She cradled him in her arms and rocked him like a baby.

Since that day, Hamed has refused to go to school. "What is the use?" he says. "Suicide bombers don't need an education." He alternates between being the right-hand man for his parents, doing chores on the farm, and being the baby curled up on his mother's lap, staring at the wall.

"I am going to be a suicide bomber" he says with conviction, striking terror in the hearts of his parents.

■ *Jill Damti Feingold*

Jill Damti Feingold was born in Portland, Oregon and raised in Israel on a kibbutz and in a city. She served as an officer in the Israeli army and has worked with dolphins and juvenile delinquents. Jill studied film and televi-

sion at Tel Aviv University. She is a dancer, and for the past sixteen years has performed worldwide with her deaf husband, Amon Damti.

AFRAID TO DIE BUT STILL BELIEVE IN PEACE

About two months before the Intifada, Amnon and I went out to Ramallah for the ending of the Human Rights Film Festival Tel Aviv Ramallah, a documentary film festival sponsored by Amnesty International. It was held in both Tel Aviv and Ramallah, but the organizers, who were from both cities, wanted to host a festive ending in Ramallah. The films were directed by Jews, Arabs and different people around the world who cared about basic human rights.

I was the associate director of a film on the stolen Yeminite children. Amnon is an amazing deaf dancer; the best deaf dancer in the world, and for many years a soloist for Sound & Silence. We perform together all around Israel and all around the globe. Amnon is also my husband, the father of our two children.

So we dressed up for the festival and were on our way in a minibus with journalists and filmmakers from around the world, including Uri Avneri and Mahmud, an Israeli Arab who has a company for extras in film. We were very excited; it was our first time in Ramallah. As soon as we got to the court of the church, where the festival was to take place, we heard shouting and saw many, many young men coming into the court, shouting and burning shirts.

I turned to Mahmud and asked, "What are they shouting?"

"Death to the Jews" was his terrified answer. "And I'm in a worse situation than you, because I betrayed them, in their eyes. Just speak English."

Well, anyway, to Amnon I speak sign language. We were told to run into the church. We got in and the doors were locked, but the crowd around was furious, shouting, breaking windows. I was so afraid. Palestinian police were running in and out. There was chaos around. Some Palestinian soldiers were not in uniform. Some looked like terrorists to us. We didn't know who was who. The mayor of Ramallah was brought in with body guards. Everyone was running around with small guns and machine guns, shouting in a language I did not understand. I did not see a safe way out. We were surrounded by hatred, ignorance, misunderstanding.

The festival was canceled. The Palestinian organizers, who worked so hard for the festival, were arrested by the Palestinian police, God knows why.

I was shaky and couldn't use the toilet; it was too close to the crowd, who were shattering windows. I was never in my life so panicky. I saw no way out, did not understand the Arabic around me, and actually thought, "This is the end." The building was surrounded by a dangerous anti-Jewish crowd, breaking windows and trying to get in.

Inside, Palestinian soldiers were running with guns and shouting. I was deaf to what they were saying. CNN announced us as hostages. I called my sister Meggi and told her that if something was to happen to us, that she should take our kids. She cried. I asked Uri Avneri if we shouldn't call the Israeli army. He said, "If we do, we will start a war." Little did we knew that a war was to start two months later.

I saw standing right next to me two of the young men that an hour ago I saw outside with so much hatred in their eyes. I was thinking, "What should I do? How did they sneak in?" Next to me was a huge tray of pizzas for the festival. (No one had the appetite to eat them.) I picked up a small pizza in each hand and gave one to each of them. They grabbed them and ran outside. "Just two starving mad boys." That's all I could think.

It took the soldiers three hours and three tries to get us out of the church into the vans. They had to push the raging crowd away from us with their guns and run beside the minibus on both sides, and with jeeps in front and behind us. My head was down between my knees. Once when I lifted it up someone spat at me but hit the window and someone else threw a rock. My head went back down as I just prayed to get out.

When we were away from the crowd, the very confused and shocked driver stopped, waiting for the escort. I screamed at him, "Continue! Continue!" He did. When we were out of the area, everyone was trying to calm down in different ways, mostly calling home. That was when the Dutch judge told us who the winner of the film festival was. She never had the chance to announce it earlier. The winner was an Arab filmmaker who made a film about a simple man and his civil rights.

The angry Palestinian mob did not even realize that some of the filmmakers were theirs, and that they were fighting for Palestinian rights in the way they knew how, through film and art, not through violence, and that we all came in the name of humanity. All of us believed in fighting for the rights of all, but the crowd just saw us as Jews and wanted us dead. (We could have been murdered, just like the two soldiers who were lynched three months later in the exact same place.)

I am very afraid, but I still believe in individuals, just like me, from both sides, who still have hope and are optimistic for better and healthier days, through film and art, not through violence.

■ *Ali Samoudi*

Ali Samoudi is a Palestinian journalist, born and raised in the town of Jenin in the West Bank. Mr. Samoudi is a cameraman for Reuters News Agency. He also runs an independent press office in Jenin, known as Al-Majd Press. His footage, especially following the Jenin invasion in April, was broadcast on numerous news stations around the world, most notably on CNN, BBC and Al Jazeera. Mr. Samudi was wounded by a tank shell on September 11, 2001 as he filmed an Israeli army incursion into Jenin. He was hospitalized for three months.

This story, written in Arabic, was translated by Ramzy Baroud.

SIMPLY SEEKING FREEDOM

When the Israeli army attacked Jenin in early October of 2002, I wasn't the least surprised. We knew too well that the Israeli army was about to launch a large scale attack on our refugee camp. They had an old animosity toward Jenin. Needless to say, the camp has been a painful reminder to Israel of how costly its military occupation can be. In the months before the invasion, that point was stressed repeatedly. From late February until early March, nearly a month before the April invasion, Israeli troops killed twelve civilians and seven police officers. One of those killed was a child, and another was disabled. The occupation army, too, paid a hefty price, for they lost five of their soldiers in the narrow alleyways of the camp, as they faced fierce resistance, legendary resistance may I say. Resistance fighters managed to disable several tanks and armored vehicles. The Israelis admitted so. The refugees kept on fighting, no matter how high the price was for them. It was like having nothing else to lose: no jobs, no freedom, no rights whatsoever. That and the ceaseless fear that death might just be around the corner.

I recall these moments so vividly as we sat and waited for the Israeli army to arrive. Resistance fighters were working together in unity to deliberate their strategy in a battle they knew would be most decisive. There were fighters from *Fatah's* military wing, from *Izz al-Din al-Qassam*, the military wing of Hamas, and the Jerusalem Brigades, the armed wing of the Islamic Jihad Movement. There were also fighters from the Democratic Front, and the Popular Front for the Liberation of Palestine. These groups, or at least some of them, are the ones that often champion the resistance, face the advancing Israeli tanks, but also declare responsibility for suicide bombings inside Israel. Israel was saying that their crack-down on the camp was in retaliation to suicide bombings. But we knew that the Israeli reasons spelled out by its media were nothing but mere propaganda. The suffering of the refugee camps at the hands of the Israeli army goes beyond two years of uprising. The brutality goes all the way back to the late 1940s, when most of the refugees of Jenin were forced out of their towns and villages at gunpoint. These villages are now located in today's Israel, yet the refugees of Jenin still gaze upon them in the distance with sadness, for many can be seen from Jenin itself.

In the first few days of April, perhaps three days into the month, the Israeli forces began closing in on the refugee camp. They raided many nearby villages. They took over orchards at the outskirts of the camp. The refugees tried to stock up on as much basic necessities as they could, using the little means that they had. They bitterly remembered the last invasion of March, where most of the people ran out of food. They also stocked up on water, since the army intentionally bombed the camp's water supply, as they often do in their endless pressure on Jenin. It was almost bittersweet to see that many of the refugees went into debt just to buy cell phones. It wasn't that they perceived the cell phone as part of their daily needs, but they also learned that the ability to contact the outside world in such times could mean the difference between life and death.

The resistance was also busy making its own ammunition and manufacturing homemade booby-traps to face off the occupation army. All Palestinian factions in the camp declared that they intended to enter the battle under one banner: "Resistance, Steadfastness, Unity." Fighters spoke to gatherings of people in the mosque or in the street, promising them that they would fight until the end, that they would not flee the battleground under any circumstances. Scores of young men offered to take part and join the resistance. However, the role of these volunteers was limited to keeping watch over the camp and informing the resistance when the army was approaching.

On the third day of April, Israeli tanks began advancing. There were dozens of them. They stopped right at the border of the camp. They locked the people in and closed down every street, every hill and every checkpoint that faces the camp. That evening, hundreds of people attended the evening prayer at the mosque. Afterwards, they gathered outside the mosque and took an oath where they vowed to resist the occupation and to fight until the last drop of blood. Meanwhile, small groups of fighters began taking position around the camp, blocking all entrances from inside.

I was inside the camp, working on a report for Reuters News Agency, about the mood of the camp and how Palestinian factions were preparing to deal with the army's anticipated invasion. I met with the leaders of the resistance and they all assured me that the occupation army would have to pass over their dead bodies to enter Jenin. I remember the words of Ziyad Amer, a leader in Al-Aqsa Martyrs Brigades, who asked me to send a message to the Israeli army, who was closing in on Jenin: "Go back to your home, because you will never succeed in humiliating us in our own land. You can never snuff out the fire of our anger and our revolution." Ziyad was killed on the first day of the battle. Ali Safouri, from the Jerusalem Brigades said, "Jenin is the capital of martyrs, it will never be defeated; because our weapon is our faith and determination. We will always be ready, because we are fighting with a principal, a principal that the Israelis can never possess."

It was nearly midnight when resistance fighters arrived at one of the entrances of the camp to make sure that Israeli snipers did not sneak in. There was the family of Abu Hassan, sitting around a small fire while watching breaking news on television. It was an unexpected surprise when the fighters stopped for a quick chat. Women raised their hands to Heaven and asked God for protection. Um Hassan called on the fighters to never have a moment of fear. "We have lived a miserable life, as dispossessed refugees, denied everything in life. We cannot run away anymore. We have to stand and fight."

I returned home, seeking some rest after three days of no sleep. Shortly after I slept, my cell phone rang. "Ali, hurry, the Israeli army is attacking the camp," said a colleague of mine on the other line. I was sleeping fully clothed with my shoes on. My family was still sleeping, as I grabbed my camera and ran out. My mother-in-law, who was staying at my house that night, asked if everything was okay. "Please take care of my family while I am gone, it might be days until I am back," I told her. This time, I was no longer sure. "Take good care of yourself," she said. The tone of her broken voice and her teary eyes were a reminder of the last time I went out on such a mission. That time

I came back wounded, hit by shrapnel. I spent months in the hospital, dancing between life and death.

It was very late at night. I had everything already prepared: my camera, tapes, bags and other equipment. One thing, an important one, I missed. How would I move around? My house is a twenty minute walk from the center of the camp. I had no second thoughts. I carried all of my heavy equipment and began running. It was of little help that at that precise moment it began raining very hard. I was just about at the center of the camp when I saw scores of armed Palestinian fighters, fully geared and ready for the big moment. Loudspeakers echoed from several directions, calling for "Resistance, Steadfastness, Unity." Fighters cheered, "God is Greater." I was so happy that I made it to the center of the camp before the tanks did. Eyewitnesses told me over the phone that at least one hundred tanks were on their way to invade the camp. But more armored vehicles were coming from other directions—from the orchards and from Haifa street. For someone who has been following and reporting on every Israeli invasion, these numbers were very alarming. The highest number of Israeli tanks to ever attack Jenin at once remained at two or three dozen. This time, there was a sign of catastrophe. I saw young men who asked the fighters to take part in the battle, but were sent away. They were told, "Your role is to comfort your families, to take care of your elders and the little children." I saw fighters embracing, fighters from various factions, shaking hands and smiling. They were once again vowing to each other that they would always be there for one another. I didn't sense a moment of fear, but mountains of sacrifice. Many residents left their homes. They encircled the fighters, encouraging them, and patting their backs. Suddenly, the battle started.

The sound of explosions and screaming bullets signaled the beginning of a battle that Jenin will remember forever. The tanks were advancing on the western side of the camp. They appeared as if they were going on an easy ride. But suddenly things changed, as the booby-trapped streets took the occupation army by surprise. The advance came to a halt. One tank immediately caught on fire. The scene of Israeli soldiers fleeing the burning tank ignited more courage in the fighters and in their ability to resist the invincible army with homemade dynamite. Another column of tanks was also advancing in the Zahrah neighborhood. There was another surprise awaiting them, resistance fighters who disabled another tank.

The Israeli army was clearly not interested in fighting yet. They wanted to create a wall around the camp. This was exactly what happened. They isolated the refugee camp of Jenin from the town of Jenin where the hospital was located. The entire camp was now surrounded. The resistance knew this from the beginning. A top leader of the Qassam Brigades, Mahmud Abu Hilweh, told me that there was nothing they could do to prevent the surrounding of the camp. What mattered, he said, was our willingness to resist. Mahmud further said that the Israeli army must have learned from its past failures and is likely to completely cut off the refugee camp from the town and the outside world.

The invasion began fiercely, with shells flying all around us. The idea was clear; to institute fear among the residents and to break the spirit of those defending the camp. The resistance was up to the challenge as they repeatedly foiled attempts by "special units" of the Israeli army to take control of the center of the camp. There was a mix of sounds: shells, bullets, booby-trap explosions and endless chanting by the resistance. These sounds echoed throughout the camp for days.

The Israeli army began its invasion with the murder of a Palestinian nurse. I learned about the shooting of the nurse on my cell phone. I tried to get to her, but couldn't. She was wearing white and a Red Crescent Society badge when Israeli snipers, perched on the top of a mosque showered her with bullets. She bled to death. Near her was her sister, who was severely wounded, but managed to survive to tell me the painful story. I tried to go back to the hospital to report on her death, but the streets were blocked. I received a call from Reuters, telling me to be careful, for the Israelis, this time, were determined to prevent journalists from documenting this story. But not for a second did I consider leaving. I was present at the first face-to-face battle between fighters and Israeli soldiers.

Leading the resistance was Ziyad Amer. An Israeli soldier was killed. Ziyad was about to leave the battleground when his rifle fell. As he ran back to retrieve it, a sniper gunned him down. Snipers were taking over the refugees' homes. They used to gather all people in one room, beat them and abuse them, as others were stationed on the rooftops with clear orders to shoot anything that moved. The third victim was nine-year-old Mahmud Hawashin. He was shot in the head and died while the ambulance driver stood for an hour, imploring soldiers to give him access to the wounded child. Mahmud, along with many other victims in the following days, remained in his home for days.

The entire camp was now engulfed in darkness, as the Israeli army blew up the electricity generators. But more dangerous was the blowing up of the cell towers. I was cut off from the outside, but that was hardly enough to prevent the fighters from getting their voices out in the media. Many had bought Israeli cell phones that continued to function, even after the destruction of the towers. When their batteries ran out, they would recharge them using car batteries.

All the images that I was able to record from the first day did not reach Reuters, since I had no access out. But the images that remain in my memory will always be present. I saw Mahmud Tawalbe and Abu Jandal, two legendary leaders who were later executed at the hands of the Israeli soldiers. When it was time for prayers, since no one had access to the mosque, the fighters used to make megaphones from cardboard and recite the call to prayer. When the fighting intensified, and there was almost no point of me being there anymore, since my footage was besieged with me in the camp, the fighters advised me to seek safety outside the camp. They tried to help me get out of the camp, but they couldn't. My cell phone battery was dead. For two days now I didn't talk to my family, or to anyone else for that matter. But there was a rumor that I was shot dead. The rumor was reported in the media and caused hundreds of people from human rights organizations and local journalists' unions to hold a march in my honor, like a symbolic funeral. They marched, chanted and wept as they carried banners and large framed photographs of me. But finally I managed to reach the outskirts of the camp, to an area where I was able to make a telephone call.

But still I was not able to call my family, for all the phone lines in our neighborhood and surrounding neighborhoods had been destroyed. I was perhaps the only journalist that was in Jenin at that point. Reporters from Al-Jazeera and various international news agencies tried to get hold of me, asking for help to access the camp. I was still inside the camp, but in a somewhat safer area. I could still hear the chants . . . "God is Greater. . ." and calls to prayer right on time. There were also the explosions. Not for a moment did they cease. But I guess that more painful than the explosions were the telephone calls I received on my now charged cell phone, people asking me to help them evacuate seriously wounded loved ones, or to clear the bodies of loved ones who were killed. The wife of Nasser Abu Hatab called me more times than I can recall, asking me to help in burying the body of her beloved husband, who was gunned down by a sniper. There was nothing that I could do. After all, my family was still mourning my death.

I took advantage of my location. My motive was no longer to get the images out to Reuters, which I did eventually, but to provide directions and urgent help to ambulances from the Red Cross and Red Crescent, advising them how and when to enter the camp. But now the ambulances themselves were under fire, and the main headquarters of the Red Crescent was shelled. I made calls to everyone that I thought might be able to help: rights groups, hospitals, charities, Arab Knesset members and the media. I demanded that they do something. I told them that Israel was perpetrating a massacre in the camp, that the hospital was filled with bodies, that corpses were laying in the streets and in peoples' homes.

A Palestinian family was then hosting me. They provided me with everything I needed. They allowed me to use their phone, which now became the center of communication for world-wide media. I stayed with them for days. I lived with them as a member of the family. We shared the crumbs of bread that were left and the light of a few candles which they bought in preparation for these days. They refrained from using their cell phones and gave me all their batteries. I did lots of filming from the courtyard of their home. True, it is all memories now, but I can hardly forget their ten-year-old son who worked as my personal secretary, answering the phone, taking notes, and watching for Israeli helicopters. I asked him once, "Aren't you scared?" The ten-year-old boy replied angrily, "Scared of what?"

More news was coming in. Most of the camp was now under the army's control. There were more dead and wounded and yet no one was allowed in or out. The residents of the camp now had a new role: they were forced to be human shields. The Israeli army would no longer take a step in any direction without having several Palestinian women or children walking in front of them. I was angry. I was sad. Yet I was too consumed with getting the word out to dwell on my anger or sadness. But now I was less informed of what was going on. Many of the fighters' cell phones were shut off, not only because the batteries had died, but because the Israeli helicopters managed to pinpoint their locations, using the signals of these phones. Several of the fighters were assassinated that way.

I still do not understand how someone could stay without sleep all of this time. But I hadn't slept since the beginning of the invasion. On the sixth night, I entertained myself with counting the missiles that were fired into the camp from the Israeli army, one hundred and twenty-two to be exact. When a missile falls, you feel that the whole world is trembling. I knew that the sixth night must be the last night. This tiny camp could not survive one hundred and twenty-two missiles in one night, I thought. I managed to get a few hours of sleep. I woke up and there it was. The chants from the center of the camp were resounding again: "Resistance, Steadfastness, Unity." The Israeli army was yet to take over the center of the camp. I wish I hadn't departed the center, but then I thought being there would have meant that none of this news would have made it to the outside world. I used to spend hours writing by the light of one small candle, then dictating the report to newspapers over the phone.

On the seventh day, I reached my home between the camp and the town. My family was in miserable condition. My wife, who has diabetes, was wearing black. There I was, a dead man walking.

For a few days we remained in a state of not knowing what was happening in the camp, yet we were sure that something catastrophic had taken place. Most of this reality I managed to convey through images of the survivors I interviewed. It was several days before I was able to see these realities first-hand; the images that crowded my mind are too heavy for a lonely cameraman to handle: Kamal, a young boy who was mentally ill, half of his body crushed to the ground. His flesh was level with the earth, with the chain marks of the tank that ran over him. The scene of the mass grave, and the weeping mothers and fathers embracing the bodies that were wrapped in white sheets, as if each martyr was their own child.

I remember as I sat next to my colleague, Walid al-Omari, an al-Jazeera reporter in the West Bank. We were both speechless. The amount of destruction we saw as we snuck into the camp, breaking the Israeli siege, is beyond comprehension. Hundreds of homes were leveled to the ground. Columns of smoke rose to the heavens. Bodies, lots of them, many burned so badly that they could not be identified, and many shot. The residents of the camp were out of food and water, but they hardly asked for any when they saw us. "Please help me take my husband out of the camp," a woman would ask, referring to the decomposed body of a once handsome man.

I was pondering all of this in my home, this round with plenty of time to express my unrelenting rage and unbearable grief. Then my cell phone rang, a friend shouted in a panic stricken voice, "Ali, get your camera right away and get out of the house!" I did not ask him for more details, nor did he want to elaborate. I took my camera, turned it on and ran. I was barefoot as I opened the door and took to the street, trying to find what my friend wanted me to see. And there they were . . . hundreds of people, an ocean of women, children and old men, all carrying white flags, with dusty faces and teary eyes. They passed by me, and with them passed a cloud of dust. The weeping voices continue to invade my memory until this day. They were not defeated nor did they lose the battle. They were simply seeking freedom.

■ *Eyal Dimant*

Eyal Dimant was born in Tel Aviv, Israel in 1976. At age twelve he moved with his family to New Jersey, where he attended middle school and high school. At age eighteen Eyal returned to Israel to serve in the IDF. He spent two out of his three years of service in the Gaza strip. He has since returned to the States and participated in various Israeli-Palestinian peace initiatives. Most recently Eyal has been working on a feature length documentary on the Israeli-Palestinian conflict.

ASSIGNMENT: GREEN LINE

While discussing the path that his documentary about Israel, the Palestinian territories, and the occupation should take, a friend brought to my attention his view that the absurd reality of the situation is that the Palestinians are not being occupied by an army of blood thirsty, nationalist war machines, but are being overrun by an army of children serving blindly a blood-thirsty, nationalist, war hungry government. This made me think back to a time in my military service that resembled more a summer camp experience in rural upstate New York than a duty I was performing for the country I call home.

It was during my time in Gaza during a small portion out of my two years in the southern part of the strip. My unit's job was to protect the kibbutzim and towns right outside the strip in the green line—Israel proper. We would do this by randomly lying behind a tree or a bush somewhere near an electronic detection fence which encompasses the entire strip, and using the most advanced thermal optic system we had, would chain smoke and play cards in order not to fall asleep.

After deciding that much like pre-calculus math, this was a futile attempt by our officers to get us to waste twelve hours a day in which we could otherwise be playing backgammon (the dice made too much noise for the ambush), watching television, or even educating ourselves by reading the latest trashy novel circulating amongst the soldiers on the base. We decided it was pointless to have all three of us awake. I mean, it only takes one pair of eyes to watch the optic system's monitor. Besides, 90 percent of the people jumping the fence were either poor family men trying to get into Israel to get a shitty construction job making less then minimum wage, working twelve hours a day, or people smuggling hashish from Egypt through Gaza so that Israelis could pay only 100 shekels for fifty grams of the Sinai weed. (Like us, who on the weekends when we would go home for forty-eight hour leave for drunken belligerent club hopping.)

When I saw the blurred neon green stick figure on the screen throw the bale over the fence, the radio suddenly broke its silence. "Amrun 3, Amrun 3. This is Laliv. We have a fence touch on 210." "Amrun 3" was us, and Laliv was the fence operator. If you think about the fact that there is an entire unit in the military whose sole job is to sit in front of the dictionary and pick random words for code names for the different units, you might be able to understand that there were jobs even more boring than ours.

"Amrun 3, Amrun 3. We have a fence cut on 210." So in what now turned into an excited frenzy from a break in the routine, we all stood up and start running towards the man, yelling: "Wakef, walla ana batuchak," which is one of the ten "important" Arabic sentences you learn in your military service and can never use after you are released. It means, "Stop or I shoot!" Its sound must give every Palestinian who hears it the same heart skip that a hippy with a "Vegan for Life" bumper sticker and a dream catcher hanging from the rear view mirror gets when he hears a police siren on a South Carolina throughway.

"Why you do this? For what you stop me?" asked the man, frustrated and a little bit frightened.

Automatically I gave him my best response to questions I had no answer to: silence.

"Yalla, you don't have better things to do?" he asked, which ironically was the same question that would be on my mind when I would be stopped for a random search by my friendly neighborhood police officer.

But in our universe of equilibriums—for every bad there is a good—the rainbow girls (the code name for the women sitting behind a radar screen only a few kilometers from us), were definitely the good which balanced our days. They sounded very sexy over the radio and their code name added even more mystique to them as they sat in a hut somewhere, watching flickering green dots on a circular screen, just as bored as us. Their job was to inform us of nearing danger: a man, a car, a dog, an owl, rain, gusty wind, and the occasional wild runaway cow from one of the nearby kibbutzim. They could tell all this by watching the dots, so we figured they weren't only sexy sounding, but probably pretty intelligent.

You can only imagine my joy when I woke up from a two hour sleeping shift to have my friend tell me that we have established a pirate radio channel with the rainbow girls and could gossip about the latest Tom Cruse and Nicole Kidman movie instead of just sitting there and watching bugs hit the loose electric connection on the fence and explode into an almost magical cloud of smoke.

The social structure of the ambush was vital to your survival through the four hours you had to stay awake. You would always hope for a good, awake partner to discuss the geo-political effects of our presence in the region.

"So, it's on 70 Hillel St., right on the corner. Aroma Coffee Shop," Saar said with an exited look on his face.

"Oh, right across from Blockbusters," I replied, satisfied with myself for recognizing a location in the city of Jerusalem, which I rarely visited.

"Exactly. So when you go there, ask for Shlomy and tell him Saar sent you. And to make you a Spoiled Burekas." He paused for a minute to wipe the drool that was slowly starting to form on the side of his mouth. "Now, he slices the burekas, and he puts hummus, matbucha, a pickle, and hard boiled egg, and it's the best damn thing you will ever eat."

Now I was starting to get hungry, and I had already finished the pistachio nuts, two sandwiches, and snickers bar I had brought with me on our adventurous picnic.

On the other hand, if you were unlucky enough to have an awake but silent partner, then the sleeper would usually be the one that suffered.

"Eyal!" I felt a nudge on my shoulder, which I had tucked under a bush for warmth. "Eyal, wake up."

"WHAT!" I grunted, without lifting my head up.

"You sleeping?" he asked.

"No. I'm trying to see if the dirt here tastes better then the dirt on 210," I replied angrily.

"Oh. You are sleeping."

I didn't even bother to reply.

But when the radio would come on and we would get the signal: "Amrun 3, Amrun 3, this is Rainbow 52, switch to turkey channel," I would rotate the dial with pleasure, enjoying every click until it hit the correct sequence of numbers. "Hello?" her voice came through with a slight hiss.

"Who's this?" I would ask.

"It's Lital. Who's this?"

"Eyal," I would respond.

"Hey, how are you? Not too many hours left, huh?" Her voice carried itself beautifully.

"Only three more hours," I said, after looking at my watch.

"You know," she replied, her voice getting serious, "we could all go to jail for doing this."

"What's the difference?" I replied.

After three weeks of flirtatious radio chatter and one incident with a fifteen-year-old kid who jumped the fence because a recent roadblock imposed on his village rendered him unemployed, we were finally invited to their hut for coffee after our shifts were over. We were in! And it didn't matter anymore: five thousand people armed with grenade launchers could come through the fence and we would not miss going to see the faces behind the voices. It didn't matter that in five hours we had to be standing in a road block checking ID cards and frisking suspicious looking old men who were trying to get their vegetables to the market before they went bad. No! This was our mission, these girls. We must know what they looked like. So, after reporting engine problems with our jeep to headquarters, we sped towards the girls down a road that only two weeks ago a pipe bomb disguised as a watermelon (by far the most creative way to disguise a pipe bomb I ever saw) blew up another jeep and seriously injured its three occupants. But that's not what was on our minds right then.

Finally we arrived, and as we walked in she was just walking out of the kitchen with a fresh cup of coffee and she was beautiful, not a flaw in sight. Half Tunisian, half Polish; the mixed ones are always the prettiest, I say. And then it happened, she smiled at me with tired eyes and messy hair, and suddenly the uniform I was wearing didn't matter. My three stripes, my gun, my vest, they didn't exist. I was a giggly eight year old, and nothing could wipe the stupid smirk I had on my face for at least twenty-four hours. And so a new routine was created. Every morning after the ambush we would come up with a dumber excuse for why we couldn't return to the base right away, and I would go visit Lital.

Today, when my American friends ask me if the army was hard, if I have nightmares, or fears that developed, I tell them no. I was just a little kid blindly serving a blood thirsty, nationalist, war hungry government while trying to meet cute girls on the radio.

■ *Nitza Danieli Horner*

Nitza Danieli Horner is a seventh generation Israeli and a sculptor and faculty member at the Metropolitan Museum of Art, the 92nd Street Y and PACT. She was born in Israel to Dina and Ely Daniely, who had two sons, Yoram and Yoav. In 1984 Nitza moved to the States where she married Tim Horner, a talented jazz drummer, and had a son.

10/14/1973

A memory has a taste. Mine makes my mouth dry:

I had a dream. No. A nightmare. Floor covered with blood. Many oh, so many sad eyes. My brother lies dead, white as can be, his eyes open, staring at me. I woke up sweating and ran to Yoav's room, " Be careful! You are about die!"

He turned over, smiled and said, "Go to bed, get some sleep. An old lady read my palm the other day. A bright future is waiting for me." Bright indeed.

Fourteen was my age and that number that forever became my fortune.

10/14/1973, ninth grade. The person who opened the classroom door asked me out. Hooray! That room down the hall felt wrong. My brother's old teacher, Mrs. Tzur, stood by the door. "Where is your brother?" she asked. At the front, I thought. The war! I forgot.

"What happened to Yoram?" I whispered. "Is he OK?"

"It's Yoav. He is dead. Your parents don't know. You can't

cry. Let's get your things."

That's when her finger started pointing— threatening and cold. It felt like it was starting to grow. I struggled with tears. "They must not find out that he is dead till we get to the hospital! The doctors must tell them just in case they collapse!" That was what she said as she continued to rape my youth with her ignorance.

I choked and followed her out. Someone came with my things. We went home and for four hours waited for my parents. My father came first, then my mom. We ran to the car with the finger holding on to my arm. My father was driving, his hair getting thin, grinding his teeth, holding tight to the wheel.

Not a peaceful silence. I feel the chill in the cabin. The tick of her finger continues to threaten me. My precious mom, trembling, hugging me. "He may lose his arm Nitz, but I'm sure he'll be fine. They say he's alive, we'll be alright!!"

I say nothing. I can smell my mom's sweat, feel her fear and her heart beating. . . I move closer to her and we embrace. . . How I wish I wasn't here.

I remember the smell of blood. I want to say "sweet," but it was not a sweet moment. Anticipation. Almost as if waiting for my parents to find out so that life may return to normal.

I smell Mrs. Tzur's breath behind my back, see her finger shaking. Tick tock, tick tock. *"Tzur"* means "granite" in Hebrew. Cold. Hard. Her authority is drying my youth.

A memory has sounds. Mine not much. As I was sunk in a plastic chair, I kept my head pointing down, trying to avoid seeing the blood. That room was identical to my nightmare. Can fear make a sound?

I am sitting alone. My parents are lost in the ER. Lots of feet rushing by, making wet sounds, stamping their way. White was not pure for me that day; it could not clean that wet, red space. Can white make a sound? There was a great sound of rushing. Voices calling doctor after doctor, people crying, people finding loved ones alive. I think of the nurses. How can they prioritize such extremes?

Help me.

A cry, heavy breathing. Is it me? Why do they all want to work here? I must be dreaming! I stretch, thinking of her salt and pepper hair infecting my wound. She looks small, but her finger continues to grow.

I had always wanted to go back to that waiting room and see if it was like my father's chair, which shrunk as I grew.

Squeaking stretchers carrying breathing bodies, how many mothers are crying? How many more men are willing to continue fighting? "Here he is!!!!" my father yells. I look and see his curly hair on a stretcher! A big round hole where his arm used to be. "You liar!" I scream. "He's alive!!! YOAV!!!"

Our hope erases. It's not him.

I pretend that I am not part of all this. I block. I'm a rock. Oh, no. Here comes my dad, punching his fist into his palm. He is looking so frail and sad. He must know that Yoav will forever be eighteen years old.

Don't remember where my mom was or if I am ever to see Mrs. Tzur again. I can hear the loud silence in the car. The neighbors all waiting outside. How did they find out?

I miss you Yoav. I cannot remember the sound of your voice or the smell of your hair after a shower. I remember our giggles and long talks and swimming across the Sea of Galilee together. Did you fall in love? Did you kiss? What was your biggest dream? Time is supposed to heal. One, two, three, four . . . It's been almost thirty years.

Don't remember much more. I was in shock. I could not cry and let go; there was no one to lean on. That rocking finger was constantly on my mind. At home I was a clown. My parents' grief appeared to be so strong I felt I would add to it if I shared my own. They felt so guilty they fought. I hid my pain and told many jokes. What else could I do?

Three years without crying went by. A young girl in a light blue school shirt sits by her brother's grave talking to marble. Just sat there, and spoke with him. Got used to the bus route and faked notes to school. Looking at the sea of tombstones, I saw images emerge from the marble. I guess that was when sculpture turned to me and said, "Do me, explore, inside are the answers." So I did.

My boyfriend one day lifted his hand, smacked my face, tired of the twitch in my eye or so he said. . . He went on and described how the teeth of death bit my dead brother's face, eyes, body and feet. Surprised and humiliated, I dumped the offender and ran away, hating him for daring to say that. I cried for so long my eyes would not open. I cried till healing came and took over.

The chisel, the clay; the travel, the play; places with no war. I ended up in New York! A place full of life, individuality and art. I settled and married, gave life to my son. Picked a place where he wouldn't have to run. At least I hope so . . .

■ *Nizar Salameh*

Nizar Salameh, the oldest of two children, lives in Jerusalem Palestine. He is twenty-two years old and a medical student at Jerusalem University. Nizar told this story over the phone to Mannal Ramadan and her sister Mae Ramadan, who worked together translating it from Arabic.

Mannal Ramadan is a fifteen-year-old Palestinian American Muslim. She currently lives in New Jersey and is a junior in high school. Mannal is very active in the Palestinian issue, and with the Palestinian American Congress. She has written various poems concerning the Palestinian issue for on-line chronicles.

VIOLENCE IN THE HOLY LAND

[Gaza is separated from Israel by an impassable wall. The only ways in and out are through IDF checkpoints.]

HOME IS WHERE THE HEART IS

My name is Nizar Salameh. I am a twenty-year-old Palestinian Muslim man. I am a medical student in Palestine Jerusalem. I was a representative of second year medical students until I resigned after the incident that I am going to share with you.

These days who doesn't have problems in Palestine? I, for one, have many. My life in Palestine is already hard. Studying to become a medical doctor is hard enough and the Israeli soldiers come along and make it even harder. I would like to share with you one of the problems I have faced. I am only miles away from Gaza. When the Israeli terror strikes hit Gaza it was a shock that could be felt where I was. After the strike on Gaza— as I remember it was 12:30 a.m.—Israeli soldiers abducted three of my colleagues at 3:00 a.m. They weren't just colleagues, they were friends of mine, very nice people. At 1:00 p.m. my friends called me. "We are in Gaza," they told me.

They said that the Israelis took them while they were sleeping, and basically threw them in the midst of what was going on in Gaza. Imagine yourself walking to school with your friends under normal circumstances and then all the sudden you are taken by soldiers away from your family and friends to a city you don't know. Better yet while you are sleeping. You think that when you are in your home sleeping peacefully that you are safe, but you are not. The Israeli soldiers can come and take you in a flash. God knows if my friends are scared, or still alive. I wondered why they took them; then it hit me. "Of course," I said out loud, "because they're Palestinian."

They had no way to get out of Gaza. It was impossible. Gaza is like a big prison; no one can get in or out. I don't know Gaza that well, but my fellow colleagues and I tried our best to help get them out, but as I said before, it seems to be impossible. Gaza is very big, and now with how it is back home, it is too dangerous to go search for anybody without getting lost or killed yourself.

I feel guilty, like I am responsible, because I couldn't help them get out of Gaza. I was supposed to be representing them at the university, but I couldn't do anything to help them. I feel like I could have helped more, but I tried my best. I resigned from my job as a representative. I think that whoever is replacing me will do a better job in trying to find them.

A few days after my friends were abducted we heard news from them in Gaza; they said they were okay, and were staying with someone who lives there. They said that it was very different from Jerusalem. There are more soldiers and on every street corner three tanks, and no one is allowed in the streets after a certain hour, and if you are out after that time you are targeted and shot at. They don't care if you are a man, woman or child. I heard from a friend who goes to Birzeit University that 100 more men from Jerusalem were abducted and taken to Gaza just like my three friends were.

A short while later we sent my friends their exams and books for them to study. We were able to send these by someone in Gaza with whom we were able to get in touch. Now they will be able to study even though they are not able to go to the college in Jerusalem.

I put my trust in God, and I pray that He will protect my friends and let no harm come to them. *Inshallah*, they will come back to their family and friends safe.

Why do we have to live like this? Is it because we are Palestinian? Is it that Israeli blood is richer than Palestinian blood?

I hope that this story reaches people in America and that those who read it have a heart to do something about it.

Palestine is our home and we know every corner of it. No matter what part of Palestine we live in, home is where the heart is. And our heart is in Palestine.

VIOLENCE IN THE HOLY LAND

■ *Nizar Salameh, Mannal Ramadan, and Mae Ramadan*

The very last time Mannal and Mae talked to Nizar on-line was for only two minutes. "NS" stands for Nizar Salameh and "PJ" for the sisters. This was the conversation.

THE LAST CALL

NS: *Salam.*

PJ: *Ahlaan* [hi], how are you?

NS: I'm fine, but I can't stay for long. How are you guys?

PJ: Fine, but why? How are things back home? *Inshallah*, everything is fine.

NS: I wish I could say that all is good, but I'd be lying. I can't stay for long cuz in a couple of minutes the electricity will be cut off.

PJ: And how do you know that?

NS: Cuz for the past two weeks the electricity goes out the same time everyday at 4:30 p.m. and does not go back until it is pitch black outside.

PJ: Why?

NS: Cuz they want to, why else?

PJ How bad is it back home?

NS: It depends on their mood. To start out with, there are even more soldiers and tanks and almost no food in every part of Palestine. My university is being filled with more bodies, you know for autopsies. There are some houses around my neighborhood that are being demolished and stuff. On top of that there is a wall being built around Jerusalem, and no one can even look out a window without getting shot at. It is really getting to a point that it is just unbearable. I have to go, take care and please, I know you guys are trying your best but please we need a lot of help. Things are getting worse every second. *Inshallah,* I will talk to you soon, but I don't think I will for a while.

NS: Bye.

PJ: Nizar? Hello! . . . HELLO! . . . Hello!! PLEASE BE CARE-
FUL!!!! BYE!

The girls have not learned anything about Nizar since this talk.

■ *Marilyn Pratt*

*Marilyn Pratt, granddaughter of refugees from the town of Auschwitz, Po-
land, left the United States in 1972 for a twenty-five year sojourn in Israel.
An environmental activist, she left Israel in 1998 in protest of the right-wing
government. Marilyn is a mother of five, two of whom fulfilled their Israeli
army service.*

BREATHING SPACE

I push the stroller and my sleepy son down the path lined with
Jacaranda. The thick perfume of the orange blossoms hangs on
the evening air. I begin the descent toward our home. Once,
when turning this very same junction with him, a newborn baby
in his carriage, I heard the groans of a neighboring Tamarisk
tree that had become parched and brittle in a recent drought.
The twittering birds ceased their chatter and a strange silence
befell the afternoon. I instinctively began to run up the path,
clutching the carriage and in that instant the dry, weakened Tamarisk let out a sickening, wrenching cry and thudded to the very
same junction, behind me. How had those sparrows known to
warn me? How had I known to run with my child? Nature has
the most articulate language, if only we would listen. Human
communication is less subtle.

I see them coming toward me on the path, and sudden
waves of nausea transform the evening's perfumes to a vile toxin.
I grip the stroller very hard and hold my breath. Please God, I
chant, do not let them be for me. This time there is no cessation
of bird calls, no premonitions from the natural order, just three
men in uniform on the path who continue past me. Mercifully I
can release the air caught in my frightened chest. "Mommy, why

are these three men so sad?" My child's question and puzzled concern force me to return to my normal pace. "Because, Ben, they might bring some unpleasant news which we don't wish to hear." The military squad— an officer, a social worker, and a medical doctor. The doctor's there to be on the safe side. These are the bearers of bad news from the front. We are at war.

Almost twenty years have passed. The noxious air is stifling. More wars, more violence, more poisonous fumes of the political as well as the manufactured kind.

I gasp. I choke. The birds' voices are close to silenced. Breathing space. I want to take my children and remove them from the toxic landscape that we call home. My community says, "Curious, you who are always so concerned with the family's well being, take them out of the promised land and bring them to ecologically sound New Jersey. What a clever maneuver. You, so involved with the grassroots movement to clean up the hazard waste dump in our backyard, now exchange one poisonous landscape for another. How ironic."

Let's cut the subterfuge. My real reason is less altruistic: distance my son from the army and his impending service. Don't you get it? I want my children to go to school and come home and grow up to be contributing, well adjusted human beings without becoming enveloped in shards of glass and smoldering metal. I am selfish enough to stop thinking it normal to jump at a siren's wail, to don gas masks in a sealed room, to take a break from eyeing with suspicion every bag of refuse left on a public vehicle, every person who avoids eye contact or makes too much eye contact, or has too much beard stubble or too few pieces of luggage or too many plastic bags and sits next to me or my children on the bus, or keeps a suspect distance from us on the bus. I want to go to the terminal and buy an ice cream cone and turn off the video in my head of the burnt-out vehicles and the scattered body parts and the volunteers that collect them into plastic bags so that, God forbid, they do not forfeit them a proper burial. In short, I want time out from all the carnage and the fear and the horror. Odd?

Is it so peculiar to think of going to work using public

transportation, feeling a sense of certainty that the day might begin casually and end uneventfully? That the end might be the simple act of completing a day's tasks without the incessant and obsessive need to listen to the beep-beep-beep of the hourly news. The end might mean arriving home without hearing names of persons I know defined as dramatic news items or even worse, statistics.

The day I left, or rather exiled myself from the country some call Israel and others call Palestine, "Good Morning, Israel" aired an interview on the environment that I had taped a few weeks previously. I arrived in Canada to look for work and to attend some lectures and so never got to see the program or hear myself speak, convincingly I hope, about the plight of the Bedouin children living in such close proximity to a national hazardous waste site that pumped its toxic garbage into our local water and air in the Negev desert. I knew firsthand about the blackened vegetation and the rare cluster cancers affecting our own community and all the inhabitants of our desert environs. But if I wish to be honest, that day in Canada I didn't give the subject of Israel's environment and the Bedouin children much thought. That day my concerned colleagues sent me to my hotel room in Toronto to watch the local news. The news depicted a bombing that had occurred hours before in Jerusalem and I needed to decipher whether the wounded girl on the stretcher, evacuated from the day's spate of violence and death, was or wasn't my eighteen-year-old daughter.

I don't believe that I am alarmist or indulgent or mad to think that I cannot remain immune from direct and painful personal loss. It seems that the longer one lives in Israel, the more commonplace the unimaginable becomes. It is increasingly hard to imagine simple things, such as a childhood of careless play for my youngsters, a trip to a movie in the city, a bus ride to visit grandparents.

"If you are not part of the solution, you are part of the problem." I thought I had invented that little piece of folk wisdom. I now felt that removing myself from the problem was its only solution.

VIOLENCE IN THE HOLY LAND

What perversion of human nature allows us to reconcile participation in any mechanism that can kill, maim and harm others? While waging a green war on those who poisoned Israeli's environment, I had asked these questions of the management of the Israeli National Hazard Waste site. As the mother of a future soldier, should I not have asked myself the same questions?

Now Ben—that child I pushed in the carriage and then tried to push out of that country—is a soldier there in Israel. He is a soldier, despite my efforts. That soldier son now calls me here in the states and there are those moments of mechanical hollow lapses as our voices are translated from human to digital to analog to digital and back to voice again. If we are not careful and we miscalculate the lapse time, our voices cancel out as we both speak simultaneously. "Mom." "Ben." He needs to make an important decision. He wants our input. His training is finished. It is time to commit to the next phase. He says that ultimately the final decision will be his but couldn't we add our thoughts and opinions to the decision-making process?

I am paralyzed. My silence is not the result of some technological gap but rather the effect of those choices, both equally terrible in my eyes.

"So what will it be, Mom?"

An additional year of service as an officer will allow Ben to continue his period of training for another eight months, but that will add a year and four months of service to complete after that. Or will it be choice two: to complete one more year and spend it performing house arrests of people who, in his words, "are unquestionably terrorists." He wants us to understand that this is a more moral pursuit than hassling innocent people at check posts. I express a third option, not one of those proffered. "Come to visit us here, and don't return." It sounds laughably simplistic, unoriginal. "What if they gave a war and nobody came?" Other countries have their haunted, mournful mothers that stand day after day and cry, "Enough." Why do men say, "No other choice," and women say, "Enough?"

So, what shall this mother say to her son? That it is im-

70

moral to have to make such a choice at all? To whom shall I explain that there is no site, no holy relic, no consecrated ideal, no people that is worth a single drop of any mother's son's blood?

It is not so easy to advise. There are suicides on both sides. Ours might take the form of confusion over conscience; theirs might take the form of confusion over martyrdom. Each confusion leaves our sons equally dead. Talking morality can certainly demoralize. Will I have myself to thank for his moment's hesitation as he opens the door to make a house arrest, his split second of moral uncertainty, his moment's pause of conscience, allowing the first burst of fire to end his life, his conscience the determining factor in his death? So this is my own death sentence too. Any advice is damning. I am at a loss to say anything. No bird calls to give me my cue.

■ *Ramsey Abdallah*

CHECKPOINT

In 1999 I was on a bus from Jordan to the West Bank, dressed as an average American. I wore a baseball jersey, a New York Yankees cap, jeans, and Nike sneakers. The bus came to a stop and I continued listening to my Walkman. Suddenly a solider from the Israeli military came aboard. He asked the bus driver, "Who is Jordanian?" and "Do they all have their passports?" The bus driver told him: "Yes, they all have their passports." He looked around and found someone that he would butt heads with, the one who stuck out like a sore thumb. He looked at me and said, "Come with me."

As we were about to step off the bus, my brother Nader stood up to follow us. I told him that I would be okay. When we got off the bus the soldier took my passport and said, "What is your citizenship?"

I said, "What is the passport you hold in your hand?"

He nodded as he stared hard at me and said, "Where do you live?"

"Look at the passport," I said. "What does it say?"

The soldier looked at the passport and said, "Where in New Jersey?"

I replied, "Do you know New Jersey?"

"No," he answered.

I stated, "Then it really doesn't matter, does it?"

He said, "Where are you going in Israel?"

"I am not going to Israel, I am going to Beit Douqqo in Palestine."

"How do you get there?"

"You say this is your country, you tell me."

He looked at me and said, "You think that your going to go into a cab and tell the driver to take you to Beit Douqqo?"

"Yes,' I replied, "that is exactly what I am going to do, and you know what? He will take me there."

Then he said, "Palestinians shouldn't be allowed to hold American citizenship."

"If they allow people like you to hold it," I said, "then it's safe for everyone to hold it."

He looked at me and said, "You like to talk a lot."

I looked right back at him and replied, "And you like to ask a lot."

Just as we began to get into it, his superior came out of the office and reprimanded him.

I then got back on the bus and we crossed the bridge

from Jordan that led us into Palestine. As we were picking up our luggage, the Israeli solider that I had argued came and told the lady who was checking our bags to search mine well, because he did not trust me. I told her to go right ahead. His superior came out and sent him back to his post, telling him he had no business there. The superior gave me an apology. It shocked me that an Israeli superior would take such actions openly and make an apology. I then realized that individuals give a horrid reputation to the majority. I felt at ease until later that summer.

I stood at a checkpoint and saw four Israeli officers begin beating an old Palestinian women. She was walking, not bothering anyone, and they started to beat her. She had a cane in her hand; one of the officers kicked it from under her. They were yelling at her, calling her "bitch" and "dog." She did not say anything; she could hardly pick up her arms to defend herself. I took it upon myself to interfere, as I was walking there. An officer turned me around and raised his hand.

I immediately said, "You know not your limits because you have reached them." I showed him my passport, and he took it and threw it to the ground stating, "I don't care, I will put a bullet in your head right now and no one will hold me accountable." His commander, who had pulled up in his jeep, had heard this and ordered him to pick up the passport and return it to me with an apology. He then relived him of post.

The military usually represents the country, they say. In this case let's hope not, because if it does, the future will be dead.

■ *Allon Pratt*

MY FIRST CORPSE

I'm not the type of person who runs to an accident site. On the contrary, I run in the opposite direction. I also refuse to watch war movies, even most of the news broadcasts, for that matter. So, I have created a very sheltered life for myself, as far as fear, mutilation, and death are concerned.

Upon being drafted into the army at eighteen, I had a long way to go before I was able to avoid cringing at concepts such as, "Go for the neck!" or "Smack between the eyes!!" I nearly made it to the end of four months of basic training without shooting a single bullet. I developed a magician's handiwork at emptying the magazines before any maneuver, and then would camouflage my impotent rifle by running close to other recruits who were busy making noise and getting their rifles sooty, God knows thinking of what, if of anything at all. Towards the end of basic training my sergeant discovered I wasn't shooting at all, and got really mad. While he was screaming at me, getting all red and breathless, I remember thinking that it was amazing how much he really cared about my ability to be absolutely ruthless, thoughtless, plain cruel, an extension of my killing machine. Though all he could come up with was: "If I ever catch you dodging again, I will personally shoot you between the legs. Roger that!!" Actually, a part of me thought it was pathetically funny. But beyond the sergeant's screams, I heard nothing else. All background noise was switched off.

Sometime during my army service I was to spend every night for six months in ambush along the River Jordan. It was a period of frequent infiltrations by guerrilla gangs, and we had to use sophisticated infra-ultra starlight something or other to target them "smack between the eyes," and shoot long rounds of fatal copper-brooches, making sure they didn't manage to do so to us, or to our families. Some guys got really enthusiastic about the job. As for myself, I was running away to classic novels and black and white films whenever possible, as long as there were no corpses involved.

Nevertheless, reality proved stronger than any illusion, and one night a gang of freedom fighters made its silent way through the reeds straight towards our ambush. My partners got so very enthusiastic, using every possible barrel, all at once. It was my good luck not to be at the helm of the machinery at that point. I was lying on the ground, among shrubs and patches of salty residue. As it was my duty to save civilians from terror back in real life I did shoot a couple of rounds, but mostly, I was holding my breath. Holding my breath and waiting. Waiting still. Waiting for the whole event to be over, as if it never really happened. But before my death by asphyxiation, one of my partners who was behind me, couldn't hold back his urge. He seized the day and started shooting above my head towards the enemy. Shrapnel landed in my lip and the salty, warm taste of blood was a great relief and an excuse to stop shooting. I gladly let the others have all the joy. When our ammunition was all gone, probably embedded in human flesh, the world was quiet again. Very quiet. And then we heard moans from the reeds: "*Ya Oumi!*" (Oh, Mom!), "*Ya Allah!*" (Oh, God!), and "*Wen inti, ya Oumi?*" (Where are you, Mom?) They died out into quiet again, followed by the howls of jackals and hyenas. Until dawn.

When the high-ranking officers came to assess the events, I still saw no real corpses but heard the moaning,"*Ya Oumi,*" echoing in my head, and the sounds of nature's sanitation workers. We got a prize for a job well done—a day off. But by that time I could not quite enjoy the concerts and museums. Even though in real life I had seen no corpses, they continued haunting me.

In 1973, the year of the surprise Yom-Kippur War, my unit's job was to recapture an abandoned kibbutz from the Syrian army. I was very rational and calculating in preparing my gear and weapons, making sure all the gadgets and means of warfare were ready and handy. I even deliberated what seat on the bus would be safest, most convenient to shoot from, and, of course, offered the quickest means of escape. Infiltrating the deserted settlement in single file, as quiet as the Viet Cong, rifles erect and ready, helmets and pouches rendering us an image of some inhuman, mute extinct species, there was dead silence and tense expectation around and inside me. But then, of course, my karma worked well again: the Syrian army did not bother to stay in that kibbutz, but continued its sweep of the Golan Heights, without leaving even a sample of a guard. It was a pleasant relief for me to realize that once again I did not have to fire a single shot. Instead, I could release all my tension through the age old nurturing job of feeding. The starving cows, that is.

The next day I was on some mission or other and ran into my only brother, who was also on reserve duty, with the paratroopers, somewhere in those cursed plains. He was shitting behind a rock when I spotted him, while passing his unit's encampment. I guess it is only your brother you can recognize by the looks of his bare butt. We were so excited by this unexpected reunion that we barely had anything to say to each other. And while busy not saying anything, he was summoned to a briefing. They were to re-conquer Mount Hermon, the highest peak in the region, a strategic intelligence hotspot called the "eyes of Israel," our humiliating loss to the Syrians on Yom-Kippur, and an impossible target to recapture. So my brother buckled his belt, finishing the job called to by nature, and I drove off to complete my mission.

That night I had the midnight shift guarding the deserted kibbutz, and I could see both slopes of Mount Hermon from my spot. The whole mountain was engulfed in flames. At times a tsunami of fire would rage across the whole universe. All in total silence. And I knew my brother was there, at the forefront of the paratroopers, heading towards the peak. I didn't even have words to mouth a mute prayer.

The following day we were transferred to Mount Hermon. Obviously my brother's unit managed to take it back, but I had no word of his well-being. My job was to patrol the vast wilderness around the peak, in case any remnants of the Syrian army were rampant and ready to attack. During the day we couldn't spot any movement or activity on the barren landscape. It looked like no human being had ever been there, for military or civilian purposes. An empty, quiet, lunar landscape. Then we were to spend the night at the top of the mountain in an ambush. Just in case. But winter was approaching and temperatures dropped far below freezing. We huddled against a rock, waiting for dawn and a thaw. But come sunrise, we couldn't feel our feet, legs, or arms, and it was very difficult to start moving again. It was painfully cold. We weren't even allowed to touch the metal of our weapons for fear of frostbite. I was wondering where my brother was, how he was managing in this climate.

     Turning back to see if I hadn't forgotten anything at the site, I saw, leaning against the opposite side of the same rock, a frozen figure. It didn't register at first. It was like a comic double take. But at second glance I realized it was, indeed, a dead Syrian soldier. A corpse. No more escape to music or drama. Death and corpses reached me after all in my real life. That rigid icy body of mine was drenched in an extreme, poignant, pinching, smoldering rush of a sizzling heat wave. Up my spine. Through my limbs. Inside my helmet. A blinding explosion of heat. So hot that it could have melted metal. There was no sound to that scene, the scene of my first corpse.

■ *Sonie Lasker*

Sonie Lasker was born in Chicago in November 1971. She moved to Israel in 1992 when she was nineteen and lived there until March 2002. From 1997 until March 2002 she worked as a senior arts & entertainment writer for The Jerusalem Post *and as co-anchor for "Jerusalem On-Line," an international television show. Sonie also free-lanced for several magazines, acted in theater, and wrote an award-winning play for an international short play theater festival. She is currently writing her first novel. Sonie also practices martial arts, which she teaches children. She is now happily married to an Israeli rock musician.*

(All names in this piece have been changed to protect the privacy of those involved.)

LEFT, RIGHT, OR CENTER?

I remember the first time I thought about going to Israel. I had just turned nineteen and my parents decided to send me there in hopes of turning me into a well behaved young woman, instead of the out-of-control teenager I had been.

     Growing up in a very secular household, I never planned or dreamed of traveling to Israel. England or Paris maybe, but

Israel? The only thing I knew how to say in Hebrew was, *"Ani rotza ciggariot"*—"I want cigarettes."

"You'll be fine," my mother said. "I'm sure there will be plenty of fun things for you to do."

Well, in my mind I imagined the desert, camels and lots of people with guns. Kind of like the Wisconsin Dells mixed with some Arizona cacti and a dash of Arabian Nights.

I was in for quite a surprise. Growing up in Chicago, the one requirement that I had for my future home was no snow. So after flying out of waist high snow in Chicago (I am 5' 10", so waist high is a lot!!!) in mid-December and landing in Tel Aviv's Ben Gurion International Airport, the dry heat and sunshine seemed to be a dream. The first thing I did when I arrived in Jerusalem at the home where I was staying was to call my parents.

"Mom," I said, "I am never coming back."

"Why?" she asked. "Is it beautiful there? Have you seen any of Jerusalem? Are you by the Old City?"

"No, not yet, but the weather is great! I am wearing shorts in the middle of winter!"

As an actress I had never dabbled in politics and didn't understand them, or the Israeli-Palestinian conflict. Twelve years later, after spending most of my adult life in Israel, I would find myself a totally different person, working in a new profession and holding very different opinions on the conflict and many other things.

In the winter of 1992, when I first arrived, things were pretty calm. The most recent event had been the Gulf War, and it was over. The only thing I knew about the Israeli-Palestinian situation was what my politically active first cousin, Rachel, had told me.

She is extremely left wing, presently working for Peace Now. When we were growing up (she is a couple years older than I) she only dated Arabs, and by the time she was twenty-five, she was fluent in Arabic, speaking it without any trace of an American accent. Having no older siblings, Rachel was the one person I really looked up to, tried to emulate and still admire. To this day Rachel is like a big sister and best friend to me, even if we don't see eye to eye. Today I am as right wing as I once was left.

Going back to the beginning, I was living on Six Days Street, named after the war, in a villa that had once belonged to a Palestinian family. One of the American girls living there worked at a hair salon, which was co-owned by a Palestinian. His name was Sammy. We met and I thought he was just the sweetest guy.

"We have almost the same name," he said. "I am Sammy and you are Sonie."

Sammy and I hung out together for a few days, but then I felt like we just didn't click.

The first place I found work was a shoe store called Parking Shoes, about two weeks after I arrived in Israel. Once while waiting outside for the shop to open, I was approached by a Palestinian. He must have been about forty-five years old, and I was only nineteen. He tried to speak to me in Hebrew, which I didn't yet know.

"I only speak English," I told him.

"My boss would like you," he said.

"How do you know?" I answered.

"You are young. You are blonde. You are pretty. You are American. Are you Jewish?"

"Yes, why?"

"Oh. Well, he won't care. You can be one of his wives."

"One of his wives?" I asked. Of course I was shocked, but interested to know what their culture was in that respect.

"Oh, he has many wives."

At that point I excused myself, got up and walked away. I mean, I didn't want to be part of a harem.

Within a few weeks I met my first husband, Aviv. He was everything my parents could ever have hoped for me: Jewish, clean cut, no tattoos, straight edged. When I first sent home a photo, my parents couldn't believe that this was the guy I was dating. He seemed too good to be true. We were married in a little over a year. I had just turned twenty-one years old.

Aviv spoke fluent English, which was important since I spoke not one word of Hebrew, other than memorized prayers. Aviv was politically left wing, too, and reinforced my inexperienced political views, pushing me further left.

A couple of things regarding Palestinians stick out in my mind from that time.

Once, when Aviv and I were on our way to Eilat, we drove through Jericho. We passed a kiosk with a camel next to it; one could take pictures with the camel. Never having seen one up close, I wanted to stop.

"Can we stop?" I asked.

"It's just a camel," Aviv said.

"I know, but we don't have those in Chicago."

Well, we did stop, and I took a picture with the camel. I was looking at the various items for sale and Aviv was talking to an Arab. I came over to hear what they were saying; they were speaking in English since Aviv didn't speak Arabic.

"Is this your wife?" the Arab asked, pointing at me.

"I am his wife," I answered.

The man didn't even acknowledge that I had spoken, waiting for Aviv to answer.

"Yes, she is. American," he said.

"She is very pretty," the man said.

"Yes, I think so," Aviv said.

In the meantime I was getting annoyed: I mean they were talking about me like an object, as if I couldn't hear them.

"I think we should go now," I said.

"Wait. I give you seventy camels for the girl," the man said.

I stopped dead in my tracks. What did he mean by offering camels for me?

"Only seventy?" said Aviv with a smile.

"Eighty-nine," said the man. He was seriously trying to purchase me.

"No, I don't think so," Aviv said, to my relief.

"One hundred camels for the girl," the man said.

"Let's go!" I said to Aviv. "He is serious! You can't sell

me!"

This story is not political, but it was one of my first experiences with Arabs in Israel. It in no way influenced how I feel about Palestinians as a people, or my own political views, but these experiences and others emphasized how different my own Jewish-American culture was from Middle Eastern and Arab culture. In America, if someone seriously tried to buy a woman in exchange for camels, he would probably find himself in a nice quiet room with padding on the walls.

By 1993 I already spoke a bit of Hebrew, and Aviv and I were co-owners of a pub in Jerusalem. Things were a bit messier on the political side by this time, but I was basically oblivious to the situation, except for thinking how mistreated the Arabs were.

We had a young kid, about seventeen years old, working in our kitchen. His name was Husni. This was the nicest kid you could meet. We hired his family to redo the pub. They were frequently over for dinner, and we treated Husni like family.

I drove into the Arab section of Jerusalem every night to take him home, and felt comfortable doing so.

Husni's living conditions appalled me. His home was on a dirt road, and from where we parked we had to cross a makeshift wooden bridge to get to his house. Even though the house was always clean and there was always food for him and his eleven siblings, there were no modern conveniences, and little furniture.

We had a bunch of Palestinian friends at the time, all in the restaurant business. Our closest were big Achmad, little Achmad and Machmud—all family, all chefs. Our little Husni had a friend named Musa. He helped out every once in a while at our pub. Musa was fifteen and was arrested frequently for throwing stones at Jews. One day when Husni had opened the pub (he had a key), Musa was there. He looked scared and dirty. Husni told me that the police had caught Musa again for throwing stones at Jews.

This was the sixth time he had been caught. Once he broke a car window, injuring the driver. The driver wasn't hurt badly, and since I was so sympathetic at the time to the Arab plight, I felt for Musa.

"He ran from the police," Husni said. "They will put him in jail. I don't know what to do."

Musa looked like he was about to cry.

"Musa," I said sympathetically when I saw him, "why were you throwing stones again?"

"Because the Jews are bad," he said. "Not all Jews, just most. I was with my brother and we were just throwing stones, not shooting guns. Everyone throws stones at the Jews."

"Why didn't you go home?" I asked.

"I can't. They will arrest me. I have nowhere to go."

"What about Husni's house?"

"They will look for me there, and Husni will get in trouble, and he didn't throw stones."

The next time Musa got caught throwing stones, the woman he hit was hospitalized from an injury to the head. Husni visited him in jail and brought me back a letter from Musa in which he thanked me for being kind to him, and claimed to be in love with me. I wrote him back, explaining that he didn't love me, he just felt gratitude for the interest I had shown in him, and that I would only be his friend if he promised to never throw stones again. I never heard from Musa after that.

Throughout this whole time, I remained firm in my belief that Israelis were not being fair to the Palestinians.

About the same time, my first cousin Rachel, who was working for the Foreign Service, came to Israel to work at the American Embassy in Jerusalem. She and I were thrilled to be back in the same country. Rachel lived in East Jerusalem, in the Arab sector. She had a beautiful home, and all of her friends were either Arab, or American diplomats.

I spent some time with them, and even though I was less comfortable in the Arab sector, I still felt safe. There were times that Rachel told me to put things like an Arab scarf in my car so that it wouldn't be harmed, but all in all Aviv felt that I was safe visiting her. We used to lunch at the American Colony Hotel in the Arab section and Rachel would talk to everyone in Arabic. We had long talks about the Israeli-Palestinian conflict and I took everything that Rachel, who is brilliant, said, as fact.

Rachel and Aviv, both being left wing, were fast friends. Aviv wasn't all that well versed in politics, but he was big on appearances and believed that Israelis who were "more cultured and better educated" were all left wing, and as such, so was he.

This is a big issue in Israeli culture. Most of the people are very politically oriented. A lot of the media is left wing, thinking the right wing people are all either very primitive or just religious. The more prevalent secular community frowns upon the religious sector in Israel, who are viewed as obnoxious, sexist and just not integrated into modern society.

Truthfully, there is no difference between the religious Jews and our Jewish ancestors, but modern Israeli culture tries to emulate American culture in every way. Just like New York has Little Italy and Chinatown, Israel is sort of a "Little America." They want to appear westernized. A lot of them try so hard to put the stigma of "religious Jew" behind them that they can't stand to be in the same area as "these primitive people who can't seem to grasp what century we are in." This type of politics is part of everyday Israeli life, where deep divisions exist between the secular and the religious, the Ashkenazi and the Sephardi, the left wing and the right.

Take soccer, for example. I am a huge Beitar Jerusalem fan. I always have been. Their football stadium, Teddy Stadium, was right across the street from my flat in Jerusalem where I lived for years. Beitar is notorious for being a right wing football club. I never knew this—surprise, surprise— being the political genius I was.

There are two football clubs in most major cities. Beitar or Maccabbi, and Hapoel. Maccabi fans are mostly Ashkenazi; some are left wing, but the majority are right wing, or supporters of the center parties. Beitar fans are stereotypically right wing and Sephardic: simple people who work in the *Shuk Machne Yehuda* (the local market), live in Jerusalem and raise large families. Not that Beitar fans are only this type. A portion of their fans are Ashkenazi, journalists and media types. Beitar is even named after the famous historical right wing youth movement founded by Zionist philosopher Ze'ev Jabotinsky.

Hapoel (the Laborer), our mortal enemy, has primarily left wing fans. They wear red, carry flags bearing pictures of communist leaders and claim to be far more cultured, educated and modern then their Beitar counterparts.

Why am I going into all this? You may be wondering, "Am I about to get a course in Israeli football?" No. The reason is that football, a major part of my life, became my political classroom, but I'll get into that later.

After I divorced my husband, moved to Tel Aviv and became immersed in the Israeli culture, I became more independent and these nuances became more apparent to me.

I had made *aliyah* [immigration of Jews to Israel] in 1992, but it was in 1997 when I started to work for *The Jerusalem Post* as an arts and entertainment writer that I felt I had become an Israeli. Funny as that sounds, it was during my time at the *Post*, an English language paper, when I truly became the person I am today. It took about five years of uninterrupted living in Israel for me to begin to feel like I was no longer just a Hebrew-speaking American.

In the beginning, one feels like a Zionist making the "big move," or maybe like you're going on extended holiday or studying for a semester abroad, but in my experience a few months or a year of being an American in Israel does not give a true picture of what it means to live in this country. For good and bad, Israel is an amazing place, full of beauty and nature and industrious people who are willing to live in an unstable economy with danger at every turn.

People visiting for a month or so haven't experienced the love of the country in the truest way. Maybe they were there for a homicide bomb or a few terrorist attacks, but that is not living in daily reality. The daily reality is not being able to be open to people that a few years ago might have been friends. The daily reality is to know what it is like to be afraid, to wonder why I, as an individual, can be hated by an entire race of people just because I am Jewish—and even more frowned upon for being an American born Jew. Even with all of this I loved living in Israel. Not having to lock my door at all times, and the openness of the Israeli people.

In 1998 I moved to Tel Aviv, to a trendy little neighborhood called Florentine. At the time I was still at the *Post*, trying to pursue an acting career, and playing the guitar with my Israeli band. I was looking for freedom. For the first time in my life, I was on my own. No parents, no husband, no restrictions. I loved it.

Little by little, as I became more involved with the Tel Aviv "scene," I started hearing a divergence of political views. You see, the Tel Aviv artist types love to philosophize about how the current government should be handling the Israeli-Palestinian conflict. They romanticize it, without ever thinking about the consequences. Again, this is a generalization, not a blanket statement.

I remember a debate that I held with my agent and another Israeli actress about the peace talks. My agent, Yardena, and the actress, Tali, were two of my closest friends.

"I feel so sorry for the Palestinians," said Tali.

"Don't you feel sorry for the whole situation?" I asked.

"I think that we should be giving up all of Jerusalem," said Yardena.

"Why, just because we live in Tel Aviv?" I asked.

"I read a story about a little Palestinian boy who couldn't go to school because he was living in a refugee camp," Tali explained. "I want to make it so that everyone can go to school."

This is the kind of talks that I had with the Tel Aviv-SoHo bunch. Tali would rhapsodize for hours about one poor little boy, Yardena would accuse me of not being open minded, and I would ask them hypothetical questions that none of us could answer.

The more I talked with these people, the more I felt lost and afraid. Where was Israel going? What did our future as a country—the size of a key chain—hold? What did I believe in? Not me—Rachel's cousin or Aviv's wife—but me, Sonie. This is when I began to think for myself. To ask questions. What was Oslo really about? What does Arafat want? Why are these people trying to kill us?

Back to football, and my real course in politics. As a Beitar fan, and working by now for the Sports Network covering football and basketball, I was always laughed at by my colleagues for a few reasons. First of all, our club is no Manchester United, and we are always about to be bumped from our Israeli premier league, but Beitar fans are a loyal bunch. The more we would debate about the merits of our football teams, invariably the more political the discussions got. Rare is the left wing Beitar fan.

At every match we went to, the Beitar fans would talk about how the Palestinians are terrorists. Now this group is a bit more fanatic than I am, but matches were always a somewhat political and colorful experience. Beitar fans would yell across the pitch at the rival clubs' fans, insulting each other's teams, players, political beliefs and even the companies that sponsor the clubs.

I loved going to matches. Here I learned what left and right wing means to everyday Israeli life—to the people who worked in the market, in the factories and kiosk shops. Sort of a politics 101 class for the non-politician.

In January of 2000, my father passed away. He always dreamed of moving to Israel and making *aliyah*. He would call me in the middle of the night, asking me about different neighborhoods, different house prices. I was living his dream. I was an Israeli. My Hebrew at this time was better than my English.

I went back to America for his funeral and stayed for two months. Everything around me—the shops, the restaurants, the people, even the driving—seemed foreign to me. Looking through the eyes of an Israeli, everything looked bigger than life, clean and affordable. Also, I could buy as many bags of Cheeto's as I wanted.

The changes in me were apparent in every fiber of my being. From my clothing, my hand gestures and the food I ate to the blunt way of speaking that characterizes the stereotypical Israeli. My family told me that my English was accented; words tended to escape me, I remembered them in Hebrew. I spoke British English instead of American, using words like que, w.c.

and rubbish.

I saw that the life-style I left was completely different. My transformation had turned me into a foreigner in the country of my birth. I am an American, that will never change, but I am also an Israeli. I hold two passports, two citizenships and in a way two identities, both of which I take very seriously.

Losing my father was devastating. My whole sense of self changed, and I retreated further into my Israeli identity. I immersed myself as far as I could go. I rarely spoke in English, even when Israelis tried to talk to me in English, I would insist on Hebrew. The only English I used was when working or talking to my family. My one American friend, Lisa, was almost as Israeli as I was. Our conversations were half in Hebrew most of the time, a language that we call "Hebrish."

After coming back home from the USA in March, I went to a press conference for an Israeli rock band. I had never covered Israeli music before, only American and British, but I thought, why not?

This is where I met my current husband, Yoav. He is the guitarist of the band that I interviewed. Yoav is right wing and, like most Israelis, is extremely political and very well informed. He watches the news every day, and as we walk down the street, he will stop to look at newspaper headlines at the corner shops. He taught me all about the history of Israel and the meaning of what is now going on. As he is also an avid Beitar fan, we got on like glue.

I found that Yoav was a veritable fountain of information. We don't always agree completely, but he will always explain— with examples based on history and current events— why he believes what he does.

He always lets me make up my own mind. After we moved in together in June of 2000, things started to deteriorate on the security front. Within a year there were more and more terrorist attacks. More and more people were dying.

I went from being unafraid of driving on my own into the Arab sector, to being afraid to ride a bus in my own neighborhood. I was afraid to go into a mall. My mother and stepfather were calling every day, begging us to come home.

By February of 2002 I rarely left the house except to go to Yoav's concerts when he played in Tel Aviv, to the supermarket and to karate class. All of these activities were within walking distance, about ten minutes from home.

Finally in March I made the hardest decision that I have ever made. Yoav was going on a nine-month world tour with his band, and I decided to come back to America to live with my parents. At thirty years old I left a high profile career as a journalist and an anchor on a television news show. To top it off, at least once a month I would get a high paying acting job—high paying by Israeli standards. I left this, my own flat, and the country I called home for twelve years to live with my parents, and maybe find work as a server.

Not that I am unhappy being here. I love America. I haven't lived in the same country with my mother for years, and my stepfather treats me like his own child. Now Yoav has finished his tour and is living with me in America.

Even with these comforts, I miss Israel desperately. I miss my husband's family. I miss my home. I miss hearing Hebrew. I even miss the disorderly life and having to scrape together to pay our rent and extensive credit card bills. I miss going to football matches and watching Beitar loose.

Now we only hear over the phone, or see on the net, which club beat them and by how much.

I don't know what the future will bring me. It is now March of 2003. We are terrified of what the war will bring. My sister-in-law has just had a baby boy, my husband's nephew is going to have his bar mitzvah in May, and I have no clear picture of my own future. As I sit here and write this, my husband's family in Israel carries gas masks and sleeps in the bomb shelter. They are in daily fear of homicide bombers.

I know I want to go home someday. All of our furniture, and most of our stuff is in storage with Yoav's parents. My question is, what will home be like? Will the terror always be there? Will there be a chemical war? What will have happened between now, while I am writing and the time that you are reading this?

Left, Right or Center?

Will Israel be the same?

I have, not by my own choice, become a political being. Everyone in America who knows that I am an Israeli—and I am an Israeli—asks about politics and the Israeli/Palestinian conflict.

Other people can't know what it means to live in Israel. They can't know how it feels to be in constant terror. Even September 11, as devastating as it was, is only a taste of what we live with on a daily basis.

I realize that I am not the left wing person I thought I was. Not that I don't want peace—I do. I wish there could be peace between us. If for even one minute I believed that giving the Palestinians a state inside of Israel would stop the mutual killing, I would say, "Take it on a silver platter." But the truth is I no longer trust that this would bring peace. Arafat has always been honest about what he expects, but we didn't want to believe it.

He has always said that he wants all of Israel. When we said, "Here, take Gaza, take East Jerusalem, take Ramallah," he said, "Sure, I'll take it." However, he never said that he would just give up on trying to gain the rest of Israel and turn it into Palestine. Arafat will not stop. He never said he would, and the Arab people will not be happy as long as there are Jews around. What does that mean for us?

If I want to go through Arafat's version of Israel, from one city to another, will I have to go through passport control? Why separate the country? What will happen to America if the only democratic ally in the Middle East is annihilated? There are those who say we are oppressing a people. But how is that the case? The Jews are a people that have been oppressed for generations and managed to persevere despite that and reestablish an independent, democratic state on the ruins of its ancient homeland in a small corner of the Middle East.

Still, as a race we persevere. We are the oldest living race in existence today and our one home is about eight hours from *eilat* to *kiryat shmona*. We occupy just a small percent of the Middle East. Why do we have to separate our tiny country?

VIOLENCE IN THE HOLY LAND

There are some who say that we are living on conquered land, that half of Israel doesn't belong to us, and should be "given back." But should America give California back to Mexico? And should Mexico give it back to Spain, and should Spain, in turn, give it to the native Americans? Should we return our entire country to the native American people? Do we know for sure which part of the Soviet Union was once Poland or the Ukraine? Shouldn't we look in our own backyard before condemning Israel, only because it is in the news? If what is won in war is considered to be part of the country that won it, why must it be different for Israel?

These are the questions that I have been posing to myself. That I believe in right wing policies more than left wing does not make me primitive. It does not make me a racist. It does not make me less educated or less cultured than a left wing journalist. I don't hate a people. I don't think the Palestinians should all die. I don't think they are inherently evil, but I have no trust in the way that the "peace talks" are trying to establish a common ground. Of course there are fanatics on either side, and they will always hinder any kind of mutual agreement, but that doesn't matter when the possibility of agreement is based on lies.

When I began my journey, I was a totally non-political being, with no desire to ever be one. All I cared about were creative pursuits, art and acting. Over the past twelve years, I have evolved, changed and grown up. Learned to ask, learned to wonder and learned that not everything is as it seems. I think that I am finally comfortable with my own beliefs, and I am firm in them. I still don't enjoy political debates; I know that arguing with a left wing person until we are both blue in the face will not change the world. Still I hope that one fine day I'll be able look back on this piece, smack myself in the forehead, laugh and say to myself, "What was I thinking?"

In some rose-colored parallel reality, we will all get along and no one will try to kill us because we are Jewish. No one will blow up major American landmarks and everyone will play chess instead of develop weapons. Until the time More's Utopia

90

is reality, we will have to do our best to stop the terrorism.

■ *Ghassan Shabaneh*

Ghassan Shabaneh is a Mellon Fellow in human security at the Graduate Center of the City University of New York, where he is finishing his doctoral studies. Mr. Shabaneh's dissertation is on the role of the United Nations in state building: the case of Palestine. Mr. Shabaneh has lectured widely on the Arab-Israeli conflict.

PLIGHT OF THE PALESTINIAN REFUGEES

My first intellectual encounter with the plight of the Palestinian refugees came in 1997, in one of my graduate school classes at The Graduate Center of The City University of New York. In the fall of that year I enrolled in an International Organizations class. The professor asked each student to choose a topic related to the functions of the United Nations. I chose to write about The United Nations Relief and Work Agency for Palestine refugees in the Near East.

As I started preparing for that paper, I was stunned to discover that very few people wrote about the issue of the Palestinian refugees and that those who did, hardly mentioned their difficult life and the misery in which they have been living for the last five decades. Most of the literature on the refugees was about the organizational and functional steps taken by the United Nations. By the end of the semester my professor signaled to me that this paper could be developed to a Ph.D. dissertation. It was too early for me to think about that, for I had neither finished

91

my core courses nor taken any of my exams. But the idea remained in my mind and I started mentioning it to my colleagues at the graduate center, and to my family back home in Hebron, in the occupied West Bank of the Jordan River.

By the spring 2000 I finished successfully all my course work and exams, and soon after a committee of professors at the graduate center asked me about the topic of my dissertation. Spontaneously I answered, "The plight of the Palestinian refugees." From that day on I have not researched any topic regarding the Palestinian-Israeli conflict more than the refugee issue.

In Hebron I grew up with refugees. Although Hebron is not a refugee camp, we lived together as neighbors—went to school, played, and sometimes traveled together—but as a child or a teenager I never understood what it meant to be a refugee. I never understood what it means to be forced out of your house, farm, or land. I saw the parents of those refugees. They looked like my parents, and so to me there was nothing which indicated that I was playing or interacting with different people. However, I have to admit that their grandparents looked tougher, with wrinkles covering most of their faces, and a code of dress that reflected a prestigious and aristocratic past.

The grandparents were more resolved, determined, patient, enduring, proud, and silent. They hardly uttered a word when we played around them. They stood idle most of the day, thinking, mumbling, remembering, imagining, hoping, staring, and yes, the longest and hardest of all—waiting. Waiting for anyone to tell them: "Now you can go back to your olive groves, your farms, or your homes."

Now, as I think back, I am trying to understand why the refugees were so sad. It is very hard to feel how others feel, but as humans, as members of this nasty, brutish, sinful, and sometimes lawless kingdom of ours, we can imagine what it means to have something unjust done to one of us. I am convinced that the refugees were sad and mad at life because of what it had done to them, angry at fate because it singled them out for this hardship, at the world because it had stood idle while such injustice was taking place, at history because it chose them to share this land with others, and above all at God because he did not intervene to help them at a crucial moment in their lives.

In Hebron, as in other Palestinian cities and towns, the resistance to the Israeli occupation was very resilient. Most of those who joined were refugees, some were local residents. The Israeli answer to those resisters who were caught was severe. On many occasions Israel demolished the houses of those who joined the resistance. As a child I heard so many times from refugees and their families: "We are losing our home again and we are made refugees again." I remember so many of those families setting tents and sometimes plastic shades next to their destroyed houses, a signal of defiance to the occupation, to the world, and above all to injustice. The role of women in the resistance was no less than that of men. The mothers and sisters of the refugees and others were so strong and decisive.

When I started my research on the refugees and their plight two years ago, I came across the same tragedies in Jordan and in other cities in the West Bank and the Gaza Strip. As a child I thought that refugees existed only in Hebron and were not scattered around the Middle East. The older I grew, the more I learned about them and their painful life. In the summer of 2001, I spent a little over a month talking and mingling with refugees in Jordan.

Amman, the capital of Jordan, is a host to at least a million refugees. As I roamed the narrow and dusty streets of the refugee camps, I experienced misery first hand. United Nations' schools and clinics were jammed. Kids filled the streets. Old and young individuals had neither jobs nor skills. Houses and stores were poorly maintained. While I was waking in Al Hussein Camp in Jordan, a few individuals noticed me. They knew right away that I was an outsider, and some approached me suspiciously, asking if I needed anything. I smiled back and said, "I am one of you." A teenage boy resentfully asked, "How is that possible? You look rich, educated, and above all, you seem to have a future." I answered very carefully, fearing to offend him or others, "I am not rich, I am a student!" He shook his head and said,

"What are you doing here?"

In Jordan I had the opportunity to meet more refugees and talk to more. This is not to say that the West Bank has less refugees. No, this had to do with the type of questions I started asking and my curiosity. The refugees in Jordan were bitter, resentful, angry, restless, and hopeless. When they compared their plight with their brethren in the West Bank, they considered those in the West Bank to be luckier, for they were closer to their original homes. It was true, too many refugees from the West Bank were going back to their homes and farms on daily basis as workers for the Israelis, who now owned and managed their homes. But I am not sure how happy one feels when he works in something he used to own or his family used to own, less than twenty or thirty years ago. Most of the families that left these farms and houses did not leave voluntarily, they were pushed out by force.

The Palestinian refugee question started in the late 1940s, right after the United Kingdom signaled to the UN in 1947 its desire to end its mandate over Palestine. The indigenous people—Palestinian Arabs (Christians and Muslims) and the tiny Jewish minority—understood that to be their chance to declare independence. On the other hand, the new Jewish immigrants from Europe (Zionists) saw the United Kingdom's decision to abandon Palestine as their chance to declare independence. The Israeli leadership knew from the beginning that for Israel to survive, Israel must be a Jewish state. They understood that having other religions and other ethnicities in Israel would not be good for the state in the long run.

Therefore, orders to expel all ethnicities were given by the upper echelon of the political and military leadership. The Israeli military embarked on a campaign of expelling Palestinians from their homes and villages. The Israeli army and some gangs, which belonged to it prior to establishment of the state (i.e., Stern, Argon, Haganah and others), all engaged in the massive expulsion of the Palestinians. After April 1, 1948 the Arab exodus accelerated as a result of several successful Jewish military offensives into Arab occupied land and by terrorist attacks by the Argon and Stern Gangs against Arab civilians, such as the massacre of 250 men, women, and children in the village of Deer Yaseen, which spread panic among the Arabs and caused them to flee whenever Jewish forces approached.

In addition, some Israeli leaders gathered the Arab *Mukhtars* (community leaders) who had contacts with other leaders in different villages, and asked them to whisper in the ears of other Arabs that a great Jewish reinforcement had arrived in the Galilee area and was going to burn the Arab villages. They suggested that these Arabs, as friends, escape while there still was time, and the rumor spread in all the areas of the region that it was time to flee.

While in Jordan I spoke with refugees who had a good memory of what had happened back in 1948. All of them agreed that their parents and neighbors fled, fearing that they would be massacred. Some of them started telling me of how their difficult journey began. Abu-Ahamed, an old man in his seventies, said, "The week before we fled we were told by people from different villages that the Israelis were going around with loud speakers and urging everyone to flee before the army came and killed them all." He said his mother was a very sick women and his dad was in his late forties. His father asked him to take his brothers and flee first. His mission was to arrive to the West Bank town of Jenin and see one of their relatives. Once he arrived there he was to leave his siblings and come back to help the rest of the family in moving out. Abu-Ahamed's story is one of too many that I have heard from people who fled from one section of Palestine to the other. Most of the refugees who remember the havoc and the expulsion have similar or worse accounts. Some remember women delivering their babies while fleeing; others remember the sick and the elderly dying because of the difficulty of the situation. Volumes of books must be written about the human aspect of the Palestinian refugees. Museums must be established to preserve their history, stories, tradition, belongings, pictures, and above all, their proof of ownership to the land they were forced to leave. Many people still have the keys to their houses in Haifa, Jaffa, Tel Aviv, and other cities. Many families still have pictures of their houses and other belongings in historic Palestine.

■ *Allon Pratt*

EXILE

On the subway, that Latino, probably a day worker. You can tell by the clothes. They don't quite fit. They don't quite match. They are probably clean, but stained. Is the collar frazzled? And the black around the otherwise clean fingernails. And the humble look, screaming silently, "Thank you so mucho for allowing me to just be here." And walking close to the walls and furniture, more like a beaten alley dog.

Not me. I am lucky. I dress better. My job doesn't require dirt under the fingernails. I am even a homeowner. I like my home. I can afford good taste. I am respected for it. I'd die if I couldn't afford it.

Miguel—or is he José?—sits down only after everybody else has comfortably relaxed, even the black youth rap dancing his way uptown. José pulls a letter out of his reused shopping bag. It is a big envelope, with big, exotic stamps with a carefully hand-written address on it and a lot of souvenirs from different post offices along the way, smeared in random diagonals that form a pattern, itself suggesting a message. But José ignores the hardships the letter endured along the voyage. There are wrinkles of joy at the corners of his eyes. He got the letter. It is here, in his hands, despite the world.

It seems like ages since I wrote a letter. Being too lazy to deal with e-mail, I don't think twice about picking up the phone and chatting overseas. Bragging about my achievements. Complaining about this strange weather. Settling an account in my old bank. Finding out the latest news from over there. From home. From where I used to call home.

José's wrinkles deepen on both sides of his eyes as he caresses the envelope. The wrinkles reach his thick black hair growing wildly on his temples, sticking like nails over his ears. Wrinkles also plow the bridge of his strong humped nose. He is obviously going through a ritual that does not often happen. The corners of his mouth turn upward for this lonely fiesta. José's fingers carefully manipulate the envelope. The front. The back. Looking for a loose end to start opening it without mutilating this precious piece of home.

What do I look like when I'm on the phone with home? Do I also look so connected and content? Or am I still critical and angry? Look at the glitter in his eyes as his mouth slowly shapes the words written on the festive and decorated sheet of writing paper. He goes through the sentences slowly, tasting each one on his palate. Here is a serious one. Is José angry, or is he simply worried? I wouldn't know how to interpret this expression. It's a cultural thing. But no, everything is okay. José is smiling again. He is nearly laughing. He needs to pause for a moment before he goes on.

Close your eyes, José. I need that moment too. Just a moment, to conjure my own family. My brother's hot temper and aggravation whenever talking politics. He will never stoop so low as to negotiate, to talk to the enemy, to compromise. "Only the mighty survive. The weak are suicidal." And any peace seeking action on my part is a "knife in the back of the nation's security."

But José is already back with his family. The second page, just as decorated and neatly written by the family member with perfect handwriting, has some serious information. As José mouths the words slowly, he is bringing one hand to his cheek. There is a tear in place of the wrinkles.

How can I explain that my peace seeking is a life necessity for me? A reason to stay home, a hope to live. How can I live with my own conscience and let my Palestinian counterpart, Hassan, suffer all that agony? Not only was his family forced out of his home in Haifa, he himself is a typical refugee camp product. Smart, as only the streets can teach you; wiry and agile, as only basic nutrition and an outdoor life-style can shape you into; and angry and passionate, as only deprivation can make you. We were meant to be competitors, fighting for the same dorm room, for the same girlfriends and job opportunities. In spite of being the more talented, Hassan had no chance. It was a rigged game. Rather than becoming his enemy, or worse, rather than ignoring his suffering, I went ahead and fought for his rights. Demonstrations and conferences, rallies, speeches, flyers and endless discussions. To no avail. I even alienated my own brother. I was always in the minority. And I can't even blame the majority. It is human nature to know where your own best interest lies, to prefer what is similar to yours, to fear the different, to annihilate what is in your way. But it takes just that little extra leap to be human, and that is where I insist on being. I will not give up. Even at the price of giving up my home. I will not be able to collaborate with my government, my army, my people, as long as we oppress others. Forcing and uprooting anybody is cruel. Causing others to go into exile is a crime. I will have to be a deserter to face my own conscience. There is no other choice now for me but to leave and seek a different home. Now, for once, Hassan and I are on a par.

José? Where is the Latino in exile? I lost José. He is off the train. But it's about me anyway. About me and Hassan. No wonder it slaps me painfully when Hassan brings up the issue of usurping his land, and of forcing exile on him. He claims this puts the conflict at an unfair starting point. He refuses to see the fact that some, like me, are also uprooted. For him there is no symmetry between his exile and mine. They are both a crime. To which there is only one solution, which is my recognition of his suffering, my granting him the return to his home.

Now, no one grants me a home.

Exile is here to stay.

■ *Sam Bahour*

Sam S. Bahour has a computer technology degree from Youngstown State University and an MBA degree from a joint international program from North-

western and Tel Aviv Universities. Sam relocated to Palestine from the United States in 1995 to assist in the establishment of the Palestine Telecommunications Company and served as its first Director of Information Systems after successfully participating in securing an operator's license for PALTEL from the Palestinian National Authority.

He later established a private business, the first ICT-specific consulting firm in Palestine in the fall of 1997. He also served as MIS Manager for the Arab Palestinian Investment Company, the second largest private sector investment group in Palestine. He also founded the Palestine Diaspora Investment Company in the spring of 2000. Sam currently serves as General Manager of the Arab Palestinian Shopping Center, a publicly traded subsidiary of the Arab Palestinian Investment Company.

PERFECTING THE VIOLENCE OF CURFEW

The sophistication in the methods used by Israel in its systematic destruction of Palestinian society today struck a raw chord with every Palestinian parent and child.

Only four days have passed since the beginning of the Palestinian school year, where over one million Palestinian students returned to their classrooms after a summer of living under the direct physical, emotional and mental distress of Israeli military rule. For the last four days the world community closely watched to see whether Israel would lift the twenty-four hour curfew/lockdown that has become routine across the West Bank. Israel did lift the total curfew from 6 a.m. to 6 p.m. to allow the school season to start in order to avoid international criticism. But the world's eye has barely blinked and Israel is already escalating its violent practice of curfew.

Today Palestinian children and parents were exposed to the latest cruelty of the Israeli military occupation. For the last four days parents prepared their children for school, my wife Abeer and I included. Our eight-year-old daughter Areen anxiously put on her school uniform and had breakfast. For her, today was an important day because the textbooks that were delayed the first day of school (because of military closures and travel restrictions) were supposed to arrive and be distributed to the students. Areen couldn't wait for her English reading book. At 7:3 a.m. we headed to school. At 7:45 a.m. and with a big kiss, I dropped Areen off at the Friends School and headed to an 8:00 a.m. business meeting I had outside my office. As I usually do in business meetings, I turned off my mobile phone in order not to be disturbed. I will not turn it off again.

At 9:15 a.m. one of the persons in our meeting interrupted to advise us that he received word that Israeli tanks and jeeps had entered the city center and were announcing that the cities of Ramallah and Al-Bireh were under total military curfew. Israeli jeeps roamed the streets announcing that anyone caught in public would be arrested. By the time I turned on my phone to call my wife, three other persons in my meeting were already on their mobile phones assessing the situation. Abeer, who was at home with our two-year-old daughter, was frantic. She had been trying to call me after seeing and hearing an Israeli armored personnel carrier on our street announcing the closure. Was Areen in danger? Who should go pick her up from school? How could we go out, given the curfew and military vehicles in the streets? Has the school administration advised the students of the situation? How is Areen, who is very emotionally sensitive, reacting? Is school still in session? These and a hundred other questions rush to the mind in such predicaments.

Abeer turned on Israeli radio and heard the Israeli plan. The radio newscast announced that the Israeli military had put Ramallah under full curfew starting from 9:00 a.m. and would only lift the curfew from 1:00 p.m.-3:00 p.m. in order for parents to leave their workplaces and take their children home.

As if the recent months of varying degrees of Israeli military curfews were not enough violence to terrorize Palestinian society as a whole, the Israeli government created a new and improved curfew—one that would ensure that the violence of occupation would come between every child and parent.

After getting through to the Friends School's hotline, we were assured that the gates of the school had been secured and that the school day was going to continue as scheduled. Although still a little nervous, we trusted the school administration and knew that if they felt the children were in any immediate danger they would advise us. I agreed with Abeer that I would pick up Areen at 2:15 p.m. and the meeting I was in was called back into session, albeit slightly less focused. After the meeting I headed to the office for an hour of work. I had two other engagements planned for that day, a training session for the Commercial Arbitration Center being established and a seminar titled, From Re-occupation to Reform. Both were cancelled.

At 1:45 p.m. we closed our office and everyone headed out to pick up their children. I headed home instead to pick up Nadine, Areen's little sister. When we left the house this morning Nadine asked if I would promise to pick her up to go get Areen from school and both Areen and I agreed with her that I would. I'll be damned if I'm going to let an illegal foreign military occupation make me break a promise to my daughters. Nadine was waiting for me at the front porch window. She rushed downstairs wearing her new pink tennis shoes, a pink hat and had a pink purse strapped across her chest. She was ready to hit the town.

Nadine and I arrived at Areen's school a little early and I had the opportunity to chat with some of the other parents that were also waiting. In twenty minutes we all vented our anger and frustration, discussed the political situation, and we even joked that all the Israelis had left to do now was to publish a daily ad in the newspaper with names of specific people that the curfew would be applied to on any specific day.

As the end of day bell rang the students rushed, as always, to the main gate. The older students knew what was going on, the younger ones did not. Areen came out of her building with a smile from ear to ear and her bright pink Jansport backpack on her back. She waved a big bulky book in the air. It was her new English reading book. Nadine gave her sister a big hug and kiss and we were on our way. While walking to the car I asked Areen if she heard what was happening with the curfew. She had not. She told me that they probably did not tell them so they would not be scared. She asked if she could buy an ice cream cone for her and her sister before going home. After quickly stopping for three ice cream cones we headed straight home. We pulled in the driveway at 2:40 p.m. and as we got out of the car an Israeli jeep passed on Jerusalem Street next to our home, yelling through a loud speaker, "To the people of Ramallah, the curfew is applied. Anyone in the streets will be arrested."

So as the world causally watches the entire Palestinian people be terrorized by the most sophisticated form of violence possible—Israeli occupation—life goes on. And as the Israeli military generals dream up new ways to batter Palestinians into submission and strip away every sense of public and personal security, I will be reading with my daughter the first three pages her new English reading book, wondering about tomorrow's curfew schedule.

■ *Amer Abdelhadi*

Amer Abdelhadi is general manager of Radio Tariq Al Mahabbeh. Mr. Abdelhadi finished his higher education in the UK and obtained a BSc in Business Administration. He is married with three children, ages 11, 6 and 4. Radio Tariq Al Mahabbeh is considered the sole source of information for Nablus and the surrounding area.

[The following is an excerpt from Mr. Abdelhadi's diary, of which he writes: "I started writing the Nablus Diary Under Curfew *when there was not a mention of the curfew anywhere in the media, local or international. I wanted to remind the world community that Palestinians in Nablus still exist but are locked up in a curfew. I was determined to keep in writing as much as I could but the death of my father last month stopped me from writing regularly."]*

NABLUS UNDER SIEGE

The day is Monday, August 26th, 2002. Day sixty-seven in this outrageously strict curfew where over 200,000 people are ordered to stay home, not to look out of their windows, not to let their children play in the streets and, of course, not to work.

Today I stole away to my neighbor's house, desperate

for some human interaction. My neighbor Awni, who is a taxi driver, often violates the curfew to transport people through the dangerous streets of the city. This morning as we sipped bitter coffee, he lamented, "We are prisoners at our expense. Had we been in prison, we would have been fed and provided for by law." Awni risks his life and his vehicle —his source of income— carrying people in need to their destination during the curfew. "We may be spotted anywhere during the route, without notice. They may hold us four to eight hours, let us go free or give us a fine, or they may arrest us."

Awni makes many phone calls to his friends and fellow drivers to check his passengers' destinations. He checks even before he starts his dangerous daily trip. In his car he listens carefully to the radio for news updates from Nablus. He takes people from anywhere to everywhere. Risks as well as costs are higher. Even gasoline is sometimes nowhere to be found and has to be delivered from another city, at a higher price too. A taxi driver or anyone else who is caught red-handed breaking the curfew, in a vehicle or on foot, is heading for trouble.

With the Intifada nearly closing its second year, many people are out of work—all the ones that earn their income on a daily basis. They are affected by the slightest turbulence in normal daily life. The past two years have been tough on them all, but the past five months have nearly broken their backs. They have worked less than fifty out of 148 days since the first incursion in April this year, including the short incursions that sometimes last hours and sometimes days.

Awni explained to me that when spotted, taxi drivers are under the mercy of the patrol commander. They are usually ordered to stay in their cars for over eight hours, until enough cars are caught in that area. They are then driven in a convoy with armored vehicle escort to a secluded area. They may be allowed to go home after some harsh and dirty words, or they may get arrested. They may be beaten up before they are allowed to leave without their vehicles and on foot, in the darkness and under the mercy of another patrol that could shoot them while walking home. The vehicles are not to be returned until the curfew is lifted and a fine of twelve hundred U.S. dollars—plus a fee for the vehicle space—is paid. Or they might be fired at before being checked or asked any questions.

Since the curfew, people have had to go many places and have been forbidden to do so. Women have delivered their babies in vehicles en route to the hospital or at home without anyone with prior experience in that field there. Sick people have died while waiting for the ambulance that's probably been held for hours by some lazy soldier before he even checks how urgent the case is. People who have fallen and have broken an arm or a leg have had to be treated at home in primitive ways and, of course, all those who have arrived back home from abroad are left at the city limits' at army check points to wait.

When I asked my friend and neighbor if it was worth risking his life like that he replied, "I have a family to feed. We have been out of work for over two continuous months and I was broke even before that. I cannot sell the car; no one buys anything these days. My wife already sold her jewelry and spent the money on food and medicine. My children do not comprehend the curfew. They know I provide for the house and they take no excuses for anything missing, they are only little. Plus," he continued, "these people—the passengers—need the transport. I am being careful. I try to find out where the soldiers are and try to avoid them."

"But isn't it too dangerous? Your children may loose their father," I asked him.

He replied: "My life is in God's hands. My friend was fired at one time and nearly lost his life but, thank God, got away without injury. I hope for the sake of my children that I live to support them, but I am not doing that sitting at home. Yes, it is dangerous and it is a stressful job, but some of those passengers are in real need and I need the income. It is a two-way street."

He was silent before he continued. "My cousin was killed while with his children at home from a sniper's bullet. He was not on any wanted list and still got it. You should see the shock in his children's faces." He said sadly, "They had to sit, for days, with his dead body until it started stinking before they finally got him buried. The Israelis want to break us and push us until we starve, but we won't give them the pleasure."

These are some stories for the world to see, hear and read from only one tiny sector in the city of Nablus, which has been sitting under strict curfew for the past sixty-seven days. The world is watching, yet has done little.

Later that afternoon I sat with my children, who were weary of curfews and were having a difficult time adjusting and coping with their new neighborhood school. Neighborhood schools are formed by parents to get their children some education when curfew is imposed and children are forbidden to go to classes.

Qamar, my eldest daughter, said, "I went to school today without my uniform. How about that. What," she asked angrily, "do you think of a school that allows that to happen?" She was referring to the neighborhood school she attended that day.

Qamar is nearly six. She's been dreaming about going to her "real" school and reading her "real" books all summer, even under curfew. To Qamar this issue is very important. This year would be her first in school. She'd wear her blue uniform like all the girls her age for the coming six years; she would study and take homework just like Omar, her elder brother. Omar, my son, is eleven. He would have started his sixth elementary class this year, had the curfew been lifted.

Qamar said, "I took my new ruler, two erasers—a standard one and the one on top of my yellow pencil—my writing book and my pencil case. We only had one lesson, the letter 'M' in Arabic." She added sadly, "I don't have my text books this year, they never arrived."

When I asked how she felt about going to that school today, she said, "School was not that bad. It just doesn't feel like the real school, where there are teachers, blackboards, classes, playground." She went on naming—in order of her priorities—all the things she missed from the school she attended two weeks ago, even if for only one day.

Qamar's neighborhood school is on the playground of the building of her "real" school. All kids in the building gathered, each carrying his/her little chair, to listen to a lecture by one of the adult neighbors. She did not wear her uniform, no one does; parents are worried that that will invite the army, even if the playground is inside the building.

Since September first, the second day for school in Palestine, students, like all the inhabitants of Nablus, have been under curfew. Israel promised to allow schools to run as scheduled, but failed to deliver. Students in Nablus attended school only on August 31. They have been in this continuous curfew since June 20.

The incursions that started in Nablus in late March and in some areas in early April, were repeated several times in May and early June before the real occupation started on June 20. Every time carnage, destruction, and murder were left behind. Since then, curfews have been imposed and schools have been closed. It was a real war, it still is.

Qamar doesn't comprehend all that, she doesn't want to. To her, the curfew meant no summer camps, no visits to grandparents, no walking to the shops, no school, and no uniform. The curfew also meant being extra friendly with both her brothers, including the little three-year-old monster, Amid. She had to have playmates.

Like all children her age, Qamar asks many logical questions and expects a good answer from her parents. Today Qamar asked me why nobody is defending us. I looked at her, at how pure, innocent, and naïve she luckily is. But I couldn't explain. I don't understand it myself.

I couldn't explain to my daughter that she will grow up in a world that is so unfair, unjust, dishonest, oppressive, wrongful, and mean. I couldn't explain why she cannot wear her uniform to her school. I couldn't strip her of her naivete and innocence.

The following morning I woke up very happily. My kids were getting ready to go to school and my wife was hurrying me to get ready to go to work. The car parked outside, carrying

Palestinian plates, had a full tank, and the streets were busy, real busy.

I took the kids to their schools; they are not looking behind their shoulders anymore. A pleasant Palestinian policeman was controlling the traffic as kids hurried to school.

The plans to reconstruct the city were going smoothly; new buildings, nice buildings, were being erected; roads were being re-leveled and asphalted. Investors, Palestinians and non-Palestinians, were dumping so much money into the newly discovered area that had so much future potential.

Traveling was a piece of cake. All you had to do was decide on when and where to go. You don't have to get permission to travel in curfew, permission to leave Nablus, permission to leave the country and permission to enter Jordan. You don't have to spend a few nights in Jericho standing in queues until your turn is up to cross the border.

Palestinian farmers are very busy; new techniques are used to make better produce. The farmers are exporting their olives, oranges, and flowers all over the world.

Tourism has picked up. People are coming from all over the world to the holy land for pilgrimage and to see the effects of life after freedom.

The Palestinian population has stopped talking about politics. They are talking about their new living standards and the new projects that are being constructed all over the country.

My station, Radio Tariq Al Mahabbeh, is very active. The new equipment arrived; the new transmitters will cover the whole Middle East. We have no problem with finances; the advertisers and sponsors are competing with each other to buy spots and sponsor programs.

Just then, the phone rang. It was a friend who urged me to wake up and listen and try to make something out of the messages coming from army loud speakers. I was startled. What army and what loud speakers was he talking about? Just then I knew. It was all a dream.

The soldiers were protected by a convoy of tanks, armored vehicles, and jeeps. They were using filthy language, unsuitable for children, daring people to break the curfew and for students to go to their schools.

The children of Nablus had issued an appeal to the world community to have their schools opened again. Since a leaflet was spread urging all students to break the curfew and go to their schools today, the army, especially the Druze, have been searching the city for any signs of education.

The articles written in the Israeli press about Moshe Ya'alon's rage over the behavior of his soldiers had obviously been for public relations purposes, nothing more.

Like all children in Nablus, my children didn't go to school. I didn't go to work either. The previously constructed buildings were piles of rubble. The roads were still blocked; the ones inside Nablus and the ones outside, and tourists were nowhere to be found.

Radio Tariq Al Mahabbeh is still offering its free services to the public. No one knows how long we have until we shut down completely. The income and financial status improvements were only in my dreams.

After thinking about the dream that I had, I discovered that the only thing in common between the dream and reality is that people are not talking about politics anymore; they are talking about the continuous curfew and the difficulties of providing food for their children. After all, it has been eighty-eight days since the curfew started. The world is watching, yet has done little.

■ *Dan Malater*

Dan Malater was born and raised in the New York City area, where he again resides. He is an aspiring writer who graduated sum laude with a B.A. in English from CUNY Queens College. The following narrative is true, although names have been changed to preserve the anonymity of the individuals discussed.

SEARCHING FOR UTOPIA IN THE MUD

I am in J.H.S. 303, in Brooklyn, watching a film for my eighth grade social studies class. It is about Israeli culture, a beautiful portrait showing happy kibbutz children dancing in a circle, all smiles. "What a great way of life," I think. I capture the images in an index card in my mind, labeling it "For Future Use."

I am in high school—almost finished, but with no idea of what I am going to do with my life. It is June 1982. Halfway across the world, Israel is invading Lebanon. My friends throw me a birthday party on Brighton Beach. That same year, I am telling my friend Julia, "I am absolutely clueless about what I am doing with my life."

"Why don't you join a commune?" was her unexpected reply.

Commune? Where did she come up with that? Julia, truth be told, is a neo-hippy, with long red hair, freckles, ripped jeans and a funky attitude. With funky attitudes come unique and funky ideas, like her idea of my joining a commune. Yet something seems familiar about it. I am for a moment back in eighth grade, watching the children of the kibbutz dancing in a hora. Maybe not a commune in America, but a kibbutz in Israel.

"OK, Julia, I'll think about it."

It's three years later—1985. I've made my arrangements to study Hebrew and work on a kibbutz through the "Kibbutz Aliyah Desk" located in Manhattan. They in turn arrange a cheap flight for me, and help me with my paperwork. I am on a tourist visa, with full permission to work and study on the kibbutz. They work closely with the Jewish Agency, which recruits young Jewish tourists to come to Israel. The ultimate purpose in getting young Jewish tourists to Israel is to have them consider living there permanently. Barring that, it is to have them return to their home countries as ambassadors of goodwill for Israel.

I've arrived on the kibbutz. The intensive work-study program I'm on is called an "ulpan." The Ulpan Coordinator, Margalit, is a female kibbutz member who warns us to stay away from the Arab and foreign Christian volunteer workers.

"Why should we stay away from the Arabs?" someone asks.

"A few months ago a young volunteer woman was working in the factory. She became friendly with one of the Arab men who worked there. Then one day, he dragged her over into a back room and raped her."

The answer makes an impression on us.

The kibbutz has a beautiful view of Mt. Carmel in Haifa. I often go outside to marvel at it. I start to notice frequent flights of high speed military planes flying overhead. They whoosh by and a few seconds later my windows make a loud thump. It is the end of the Israeli involvement in Lebanon to oust the PLO, and the jets are returning home.

The group I'm studying with includes Jewish tourists from around the world. We study Hebrew for five hours a day, work for three, and then at night socialize in English. My job is in the plastics factory. I wait for long sheets of plastic to drop off of the assembly line. As they drop, I must stack each piece, flush against the other. When I have ten pieces stacked together, I fasten them on the edge with a bright yellow strip of tape so that they can be easily inventoried.

Most of the workers are kibbutz members. They all wear the same standard issue navy colored shirts and work pants. There are also Arab workers who come from outside the kibbutz who are on salary. They wear T-shirts, jeans, and sneakers. Outside of work I would never be able to tell an Arab from a Jew. I talk a little to the kibbutz members in the factory, but not to the Arabs.

On the kibbutz itself there are no Israelis my age, only younger ones and older ones. I am twenty years old. The Israelis my age are all in the army.

One weekend, the soldiers are home. They ask to have a shared event with the ulpan students. Both of our groups sit around a campfire, singing songs and playing games. On Sunday morning they are gone again. Once they are gone, we mingle somewhat with the pre-army and post-army crowd, sectioned off with us on the young people's "ghetto" on the kibbutz.

As the need arises, Ilan, the work manager, takes me from the drudgery of the factory and sends me off to pick weeds in the cotton field. Ilan is tall and lanky. He guides my fellow ulpanists and me through row after row of cotton plants. Something about the way he cranes his neck back and forth reminds me of a chicken.

We are a motley crew. There is a Soviet dissident, a German Jew, as well as American and British nationals. In between picking out the weeds, we discuss the state of the world, philosophy and religion. The Russian cannot go back to the Soviet Union. He left there illegally and is now traveling the world with his Canadian bride. The German Jew feels there is no place for him in Germany and wants to make a life here.

I have two roommates. There is Phil, from Australia, whom I met at the airport on the way to the kibbutz, and David from France.

Phil, as I find out, is a born-again Christian. He has kept this a tightly guarded secret for a couple of months, but now he is avidly trying to convert me with his doctrine. In the world according to Phil, it is sinful to listen to rock music, it is sinful to dance, and it is sinful to lust after a woman. The list goes on. He goes off the kibbutz a few times a week after work. He is a part of a Christian group which baptizes new converts in the Jordan River.

"You should have seen it tonight, Danny," he tells me. "It was beautiful. We baptized a young Palestinian girl from a Muslim family. The sun was setting, just as wonderful as can be, and she was crying tears of joy. I'm sure if her parents knew what she was up to, there'd be trouble."

Phil has his cause, but it is not mine. I have no objections to his group baptizing a willing convert, but I do object to him trying to forcibly trying to convert everyone he meets.

David is a short, blond-haired Frenchman with a minor acne problem. But his major problem is not acne, but his sense of style. He only seems to have one pair of shorts. This wouldn't bother me so much but for the fact that these gym shorts are way too short on him and seeing his private parts is not something I or anyone else wants to see. Poor David has now become completely identified his way-too-short shorts.

One day a group of ulpan students are in my room, discussing David's gym shorts.

"They've got to go," someone says, as we all give nods of assent. David has gone off tonight to visit someone, and for once he is wearing his jeans. We choose lots amongst ourselves, and the one chosen to do the deed grabs the shorts, steps outside and hurls them to the rooftop. David returns and cannot find his shorts. He is forlorn.

"Did anyone see my shorts?"

"Sorry, mate, haven't seen 'em," says Phil.

I shrug my shoulders.

David looks high and low, but still no shorts. Phil shows David some compassion and lends him a pair of his own shorts. David tries them on, and lo and behold, actually go down to his thighs! David now walks the kibbutz in style, but he has a vacant look in his eyes. Something was taken away from him and he knows it. It is almost as if a piece of his identity was stolen with the shorts. I finally break down and point to his shorts on the rooftop.

"You fucking bastards."

He retrieves the shorts, and suddenly the old David is back. I breathe a sigh of relief. No one should have his identity stolen from him, forced to wander the world with an assumed one, even if it is wrapped up in an extremely revolting pair of gym shorts.

Every so often the ulpan staff takes us on a road trip. Today we are going to the Druze village of Dalyat El Carmel, located near Haifa. The Druze, we are told, are a peaceful Arab folk who want nothing more than to live in peace with their neighbors. They willingly accept the rule of whatever government is in power. Furthermore, we are told, in their secret religious doctrine they make reference to a people who would "be as brothers" to them. Thus, they consider the Jews who arrived in their midst to be these "brothers." The men wear baggy pants with an excessive amount of room in the front. The Druze believe a messiah will be born to a man, and they must be prepared to catch the messiah in their pants if he is born while they are going about their normal day-to-day activities. I find it all very fascinating. I buy a small drum from one of the vendors in the town and then I never meet another Druze until a long time from now.

On another trip we are taken to see the oldest continuously running synagogue in Israel. The family that runs it has been at it for umpteen generations or so. When the Zionist settlers arrived, they tried to connect with this family. But because the family was virtually indistinguishable from their Arab neighbors, the European Jews did not know what to make of them and left them alone.

We enter the threshold of the synagogue. Efrat, our Hebrew instructor, has brought along her boyfriend, who refuses to don a kippa on his head.

"No, but why should I? I don't believe in God, so why should I have to wear a kippa? Just because I am in a synagogue?"

We are shown the exit.

"We can be Jews – but without God!" proclaims Efrat in exuberance.

Phil and I visit an older couple named Dov and Shulamit, who came to the kibbutz in the 1940s from Eastern Europe. Dov regales us with stories from the early days of the kibbutz.

"When we came to the kibbutz there were no permanent structures, only a few tents. Now look at us," he says.

As an older kibbutz, it has a great number of elderly residents in various states of physical and mental health. I am next to one such elderly resident as I scoop out the ingredients for my evening salad in the dining hall.

"What's the film tonight?" I ask him.

He looks at me and sings, "Uhh ahh!!" His son leaps out of his chair and guides his father away by the arm.

I want to get out of this kibbutz. It doesn't seem to be a place for a young single guy. Sure, I've had a good time. I've met Jewish people from around the world and partied up a storm with them. I've gotten a short exposure to kibbutz life and picked a smattering of Hebrew. I leave the kibbutz with pleasant memories, all in all.

It is 1986, and I am now in a kibbutz which was founded seven years ago, located in the Judean Desert. I am here under the auspices of the Jewish Agency. I'm on a three-month program with two slightly older South African women. We are here to experience life on a young kibbutz. The South African women barely speak to me. There are a total of maybe twenty people on the kibbutz, with just about as many dogs. No one is over thirty years old, and there are no children or elderly people, either.

I am put to work in a tiny factory, which makes one-inch parts for automobiles. I'm on my first hour of my first day of work, affixing Part A to Part B. I don't even know which part of the automobile the finished piece is supposed to fit into. The factory manager approaches me and asks if I would consider taking over his position. I don't know how to run a business, I know nothing of automobile parts and I barely speak Hebrew. And aside from all that, it was my first hour of my first day at work! My first day! I politely refused his offer. The kibbutzniks in the factory look at him as if he has gone mad.

The kibbutz members are a quiet lot. I make friends with a couple of English speakers. One is a woman named Jessica from Northern England. But aside from pleasant conversations, there is absolutely nothing to do on the kibbutz. Nothing! Not even a swimming pool to go to after a hot day of work.

One afternoon after work I head off two paces and I am in the desert. I contemplate screaming my lungs out. No, I won't do it here. I step two paces back, and I am in the kibbutz again. My friend Jessica meets me there.

"Maybe I should go to the turkey shed and scream my lungs out," I tell her.

"No, you don't want to do it there, either," she says. "I did it there, once, when a kibbutz member came in and caught me in mid scream."

The kibbutz is just down the road from the Arab city of Jericho in the West Bank. The kibbutz, while it is not too far from Jerusalem, is also in the West Bank, a fact that doesn't quite sit well with me. I keep my opinions to myself. I will be leaving the kibbutz in a couple of months, anyway. One kibbutz member tells me how great relations are between themselves and the Jericho residents.

I am 0-2 in finding a kibbutz to fit into for life. I think I need to be more fluent in Hebrew. I enroll myself into another ulpan work-study kibbutz program. This time, however, I've chosen a more left-wing kibbutz, located near the Israeli town of Afula. Dalia is a woman in her early twenties who lives in my section of the kibbutz. To say that she is very outspoken is an understatement. One day Dalia and I are talking politics.

"We must fight the Arabs," she says. "It is the only language they understand."

"But don't you eventually want to live in peace?"

"No, why should we? They don't want to live in peace with us."

"So you're prepared to continue fighting with them."

"Yes, of course."

"For how long?"

"For 100 years, 1000 years, forever if necessary."

There doesn't seem much point to argue with someone so entrenched in her position, so I drop the subject.

I hear a snippet of conversation in the dining room.

"There can be no peace without negotiation," a man is saying. "We have no choice except to negotiate with our enemies."

There is a demonstration in Tel Aviv against the Orthodox Jews trying to exert their rules on the secular Jewish population. The secular Jews believe that the religious authorities should not make decisions for them. In Israel you cannot marry, divorce or get buried where you want, without the religious authorities having some say in the matter. This is not the first such demonstration, and it will not be the last. The kibbutz rents two buses to go down to the demonstration. There are many teenagers on the bus. They each wear a bright blue shirt with a shoelace that ties around the neck, instead of shirt buttons. The shirt is a historical symbol which shows that they are of the left-wing Jewish youth movement, Ha-Shomer Hatzair. There are also many older kibbutz members on the bus. We join the demonstration, and the teenagers burst out chanting and singing. A few hours later, we're back on the kibbutz. It is nice to finally be in a place that has so many passionately left-wing people in it.

The ulpan staff takes us to visit the neighboring Arab village, which is located just across from our fields. The headmaster of the Muslim elementary school proudly shows us his school and his students. A kibbutz member, who is with us, tells of the wonderful relations the kibbutz has with this Arab village. We are shown around the various houses of the village, from the outside, and then we walk back to the kibbutz. On the kibbutz, Rutie, who serves both as Ulpan and Volunteer Coordinator, warns us not to enter the Arab village.

Rutie has been a bit of an alarmist of late. She makes sure that we each get a copy of the English language daily newspaper *The Jerusalem Post*. Just in case we miss a particularly gruesome article, such as a tourist being stabbed to death by a terrorist, it is posted in a prominent spot outside her office for us to see.

Rutie's tactics work. We are extremely paranoid. So much so that Jane, one of the English volunteers, gets freaked out when an Arab villager knocks on her door and asks for her by name. Her roommate covers for her by saying that she left the kibbutz, and the man goes away.

"How did he find out your name?" I ask Jane.

"He went around the kibbutz, asking for the English hairstylist. Someone told him my name, and then he showed up on my doorstep."

"Did you ever speak to him before?"

"No, I hadn't. That's what's so completely frightening about it."

"Maybe he just wanted a haircut . . ."

"Well, yes, but even so. It isn't every day you get a strange man at your doorstep, asking for you by name."

I concede her point that it is "better to be safe than sorry."

Once again I'm in the young people's section of a veteran kibbutz. Left to ourselves, and virtually ignored by the kibbutz population at large, we create our own entertainment. We light bonfires, dance to music, and down as much alcohol as possible.

I am shifted from position to position. Now I work in the dining room, now in the field. I am in the factory, which produces electrical wires, and then I'm off to weed someone's garden. I have had just about every conceivable job on the kibbutz. Finally, I am given the dirtiest job that the kibbutz has to offer—sweeping up the factory floor. I'm regretting my behavior of the past months. Now that the alcoholic haze is wearing thin, I'm now appreciating the finer things about the kibbutz, such as the mellow evenings in the clubroom. In the clubroom I drink cappuccino while reading novels by Hermann Hesse and Yukio Mishima or talking to friends and kibbutz members. I begin to think of the kibbutz as a possible place to live.

But in order to become a member, I must first become a candidate. But in order to become a candidate, I must first past muster with Rutie, who we on the ulpan and volunteer section call "The Dragon Lady" for her hardheaded approach to her job. More than once a person was thrown off of the kibbutz with a mere blink of her eyelash. "I am thinking of becoming a candidate for kibbutz membership."

Without missing a beat she says, "But I heard you were drunk three times."

I am crestfallen. I know that this means that in her book I am not worthy. I look at her face for some sign of compassion. She sighs.

"Danny, I think you would be better off in a younger kibbutz."

I am surprised by the glint of compassion. I realize that perhaps she is right.

It is 1987. I have been back in the United States for a short time and I am working at odd retail jobs. I'm starting to miss living in Israel and speaking Hebrew. In my spare time, I read books on Zionist philosophies of the early Jewish settlers.

117

Their dedication to reestablishing themselves in the historical Jewish homeland warms my heart. I decide I'll give the kibbutz life one last chance. If it doesn't work out this time, maybe I'd try life in an Israeli city.

I point myself back to the "Kibbutz Aliyah Desk" in Manhattan. In September 1987, I am back on a kibbutz in Israel with a group of fellow Americans who have also come to settle on a kibbutz. The kibbutz is located on a breathtakingly beautiful plateau on the Golan Heights, which overlooks Lake Kinneret, also known as the Sea of Galilee.

It was founded in 1973, after Israel defeated the Syrian forces in what is known as the Yom Kippur War. The members are mostly in their thirties and the oldest kibbutz child is now twelve years old. The kibbutz has a good balance of Americans and Israelis, and everyone seems more or less laid back.

I go through the usual disappointments of kibbutz work. It is mostly menial labor. I don't exactly have a set of career skills, and the kibbutz doesn't exactly have a wide range of interesting work. For my first job, I am placed in the laundry room. I work there for several months, and then ask the work manager for a change. I go from working in the fields to the dining room and then back to the laundry room. I never know where I'll work in a given day for quite a while. I go to work for a few months in the kibbutz factory, which produces irrigation parts.

Eventually I grow tired of factory work. I request a transfer for restaurant work in the off-site hot springs resort, which is owned in part by the kibbutz. I don't think much about the army until the news consists of nothing but reports of military conflict. Until this point, I haven't asked about anyone's military experiences. All that changes.

It's December 8, 1987. A van of workers from Gaza comes to Israel traveling to work. A military vehicle collides with the van, killing the workers. People in Gaza are rioting in the streets, pelting the soldiers with stones. Some say the Israelis killed those workers in the van on purpose.

These "disturbances" are still going on a week, and then a month later. If they only knew that it was an accident that killed these workers, I think, then there wouldn't be any reason to riot. Now some months later, the riots are dubbed the Intifada, (Arabic for "shaking off") by the Palestinian leadership. I know now there must be something going on other than a reaction to an unfortunate accident.

The images of soldiers shooting and arresting rock throwing Palestinian children become familiar sights. Now I see real life events unfolding, and they seem to be just another series of bad action films. Some soldiers from an immigrant group come home for the occasional weekend, but they don't want to discuss anything. They just want to strip out of their uniforms, into regular clothes, and then dance and drink in the kibbutz pub.

I am beginning to think about my future in Israel. I'm not quite sure I want to live in the kibbutz for the rest of my life, but I still want to be in Israel. I want at least to continue the Israeli part of my experiment; i.e., I want to know what does it mean to be an Israeli. I want to be here. I want people here to accept me. I come to the conclusion that there is no way I can know what living in Israel is like without joining the army. I dread the thought of becoming a soldier, given the current set of events, but I see no other choice.

It looms over me like a black cloud. I think back to a point in my childhood in 1972. I am eight years old. A counselor calls a group of us over during a special activities day.

"What year were you born?" an adult asks.

The student responds.

"Oh," says the adult, "then you will be drafted into the army in the year such and such."

I am cowering in the distance. I don't want to know when I'll be drafted. I'll be damned if I'm going to be a soldier, killed in some distant war in the year such and such.

It's 1988. The fear of military service and the desire to become a "true Israeli" play off each other in my mind. Watching the Intifada play itself out on TV doesn't help matters much. I go to sleep and dream that I am already an Israeli soldier, caught up in a hairy situation. I decide that I can't live in fear of the army for the rest of my life. If I give in to my fears, I'll always be cowed by the fact that I was running away from them. Plus I'll never completely have finished my Israeli experiment. It's early 1989, and I've made my decision. I take myself down to the Ministry of Interior in Tiberias, and I fill out the form that will make me a citizen. I walk out of the building and note the fact that it is right next door to the Military Recruitment Center. Three weeks later I am an Israeli. Two weeks after that, I am served notice to report to the Military Recruitment Center for a preliminary interview.

July 1989. I am heading down to the Military Induction Center with a group of other immigrants. On arriving there, I see a familiar face. It is Greg, a tall South African, from a group of immigrant soldiers who had been on the kibbutz.

"So, I see they've made you a sergeant," I say.

He pulls me off to one side and whispers, "Listen, Danny, I'm going to be your commanding officer. We can still be friends when we're back on the kibbutz for the weekend, but in the army you have take me serious and follow to my commands, okay?"

"Okay, Greg, no problem."

In fact, it never becomes a problem. As my commanding officer, Greg acts like a completely different person. He runs me ragged, just as he runs everyone else in my unit ragged. On a weekend off on the kibbutz, he is asking me if I want to join his team in a game of water polo in the swimming pool.

In basic training, my group is joined by a bunch of Israelis who come from troubled backgrounds. They are friendly at first, but this doesn't last for long. Soon there are fist fights and arguments. We are told that it doesn't matter where we've come from. We are all Israeli soldiers, in this together.

I feel myself regressing to a hostile, defensive mode, always ready to defend myself against some minor slight. I want to scream. I do scream. I fight back. It doesn't help.

Even before we are finished basic training, we are dragged into a small provincial town on the Gaza Strip. We are based in a house, enclosed by a security fence. We go out on patrols, seeking out rock-throwers. Our company commander is a stern man who brooks no insult. He tells us that if someone throws a stone, we must chase after him. An officer comes against a child who is perhaps nine years old. He has grabbed the boy by the collar and is holding him aloft against a wall.

"Were you throwing stones?"

"No, I wasn't."

The officer slaps him on the face with his free hand.

"Don't lie to me. I can see by your dirty hands that you've been throwing stones."

"I didn't throw any stones."

The officer slaps him across the cheek again.

"I want you to go back home, and I don't ever want to see you out here throwing stones again, do you hear?"

"Yes."

The officer puts the boy down, and the boy runs off, crying. Soldiers in my company are whining about the lack of latitude they have in dealing with the Palestinians, unhappy in just slapping a suspected rock thrower in the face a few times. If it were up to them, we'd all go "Rambo" on the Palestinians. But there are rules and regulations to follow, and so they do.

I can see the residual resentment that one of my fellow soldiers, Ehud, still has from being run around ad-nauseam in basic training. He takes his aggression out on a middle-aged Palestinian resident, treating this grown man as if he was a raw recruit. "I want you to run over to that wall and return, repeating the words, 'I'm a stupid Arab.'"

"It is that all?" the Arab resident asks.

"Yes, run to the wall saying, 'I'm a stupid Arab.' Go do it now."

The man runs at top speed to the wall and back. "I'm a stupid Arab! I'm a stupid Arab! I'm a stupid Arab!"

"Now do it again."

He does it again, and now stands in front of Ehud, grinning.

"OK, you are a stupid Arab. Now get out of my face," says Ehud, laughing. The Arab man also walks off, also laughing to himself. He would be here long after the Israeli soldiers were gone, and for that fact he was not humiliated and thought it all a joke.

As my service goes on there are more periods of training and more time in the Gaza Strip. We are called on to lay ambushes, and also to enter into people's homes to arrest them. When the officers are looking to assemble a macho gung-ho crew for a given operation, they generally do not look for me. I and a few other "scrubs," as I like to think of us, are left to what is thought of as minor duties, such as guarding the front door of an apartment building while the more macho of our crew are interrogating and slapping someone around inside. The arrangement is fine by me.

I'm guarding a roadblock in Rafah, with the radio on. There is a report of riots in Rafah, which are being dispersed by helicopters. I hear a whirring overhead. I look up to see a helicopter.

I am dragged into the heat of the action. We are running back and forth and a rock grazes my right ankle. I see a sixteen-year-old girl watching dispassionately from her balcony as if it was a tennis match. I lock my eyes onto hers and I plead with her, silently. Look beyond my uniform and see me for the peace loving human being that I am. I hope perhaps to see in her a shred of humanity amongst the madness. For instant she is confused. Then she makes a snap decision. Her face turns into a sneer, and she is waving a "V" sign for victory to taunt me. I look away in disgust.

From that moment on, I no longer consider myself an American liberal. My identity must be as an Israeli soldier, not as an American, as long as I am in uniform. I make ground rules for myself: 1) I'll try not to abuse any Palestinians, but neither will I excuse their violence. 2) I will feel nothing toward them now. I know I'll feel things after my time here is done, but right now I don't have the luxury of sentimentality. 3) I will not hit a Palestinian if I don't have to. In fact, I know that others will do it, so there's absolutely no reason I should. I may be numb, but I'm still no macho gung-ho soldier. 4) My motto is as follows, feel nothing, do as little as possible, avoid being hit by rocks. 5)

And finally, do nothing you'll regret later on.

When Shimon shoves an Arab for walking down his own street, I tell him not to be extreme. But I don't even have the passion to feel my own words anymore. They are just words I think I should say.

I am sucked into the game. Boys throw stones at us. We turn and point our rifles in their direction. They run away. I swirl around and point my rifle in the direction from where a rock was thrown. I am faced with a young girl, whose face is horror stricken and cannot move. I lower my rifle and am thoroughly disgusted with myself. I want to throw my rifle into the street and walk away.

In the Christian world, it is Christmas Eve and peaceful thoughts abound. But this is not the Christian world. We patrol a beach in Gaza. We are trying to be as quiet as possible. The Arab residents of the town are under curfew, so anyone we run across can only be up to no good. We hunch down, and creep quietly along the beach.

"HELLO!!"

Guns are cocked in the direction of the unexpected intrusion. Two Arabs are wandering the beach. They are ordered to kneel down. My commander appoints Ron and me to set guard over the two suspects, while the rest of the troop go off to patrol the village.

Ron is standing over his kneeling suspect and I am standing over mine. The man I am guarding shifts his legs. "Don't move." I say this in order for him to get the impression that I mean business.

The evening wears on, and there is no sign of the patrol. I am tired of standing, so I take a kneeling position. I shift each successive leg as it gets stiff, and pretty soon I am doing a Cossack type dance in the middle of the beach. The Palestinian, as instructed, has not moved.

The patrol returns at sunrise. I can now clearly see the Palestinian I have been guarding for the entire evening. He's black! How can I have been face to face with him all this time and not noticed?

The two men, indeed, did have a right to be on the beach. They are beach workers, and were just doing their job. We let them go home.

I am called on to go on more patrols. If I enter a house, I let other soldiers interrogate suspects and slap them around, as I stay in the background. I am not giving a damn either way by now. If I am assigned to attach the rubber bullets on my rifle, I don't fire them. When asked to, I exchange rifles temporarily with others, and they fire the rubber bullets instead, before giving my rifle back to me. I'm under no delusions that I'm innocent here. Kids are being injured by the rubber bullets fired from my rifle. So what that it's not me firing it.

I am numb. I don't care. I just want out of here. I want to be a human being again, to feel again. I AM NUMB.

On the last morning in Gaza we are alerted to look out for a kid on a bicycle who's been throwing rocks at the troops. Eventually, a kid on a bicycle rides by. No one in my group has seen him throwing rocks, but we stop and interrogate him anyway. Itai asks if anyone has a utility knife. I shrug, and hand over mine. He attempts to slash the boy's tire, but the tire is rough, and it doesn't work. He gives me back the knife. I am way past arguments of why to do or not to do anything. Thank God we're getting out. Any longer, and I'll be one of those gungho assholes. It all starts with becoming numb.

I never went to Israel seeking out the problems of the Middle East. I went looking for the promises of the old Zionist pioneers: "Come, young Jew. Come to Israel. Here we are all one family, and can live as Jews should live."

Or something to that effect. They conveniently forgot to mention our Semitic cousins, the Palestinians. No film of how they live was ever shown to me. Instead, I was thrust into their lives, unprepared. There are two stories in this land called Israel.

I've been back in America for over a decade. I live my American life, but I read the news and have nasty reminders. For a while it looks as though there may finally be peace in Israel. Then Yitzhak Rabin is assassinated. I feel as if someone in my own family had died. An Israeli air force pilot is killed as his plane crashes during a training mission. When he was seventeen, I played Frisbee with him on a kibbutz. In the winter of 2002 I open a newspaper and see the face of my former company commander, staring back at me. He was killed by a piece of debris which fell from a bulldozed house as he questioned a suspect in the West Bank. The tragedy of these lost lives is all too much for me. I break down crying, and somewhere within me I know that a minor miracle has occurred: I am no longer numb.

I seek to make sense of it all. I am a voracious reader of books on the Middle Eastern conflict. In New York City I speak to Israelis and Palestinians alike, to find out their different stories. It feels so far away from where this conversation should be taking place. I run a film in my mind. In this film there are children, Palestinian and Israeli, dancing in a circle, all smiles. I label this film "For Future Use."

■ *Emily Schaeffer*

Emily Schaeffer lived in Jerusalem on and off for a year and a half between 1998 and 2000, and has traveled extensively in the Middle East. She has lived in New York and worked in the communications division of an international women's reproductive health and rights organization. Emily is presently studying law as part of her pursuit of a career in international human rights advocacy.

MY ISRAELI-PALESTINIAN PEACE PROCESS

It is 4:00 a.m. on my twenty-second birthday, and I am camped out at Ben Gurion airport in Tel Aviv. I am still desperately trying to grasp all that has transpired over the past five months, to no avail. I torture myself repeatedly with the possibility that by leaving I am making a grave mistake.

Living in Israel posed no conflict for me when, six years

earlier, I had fulfilled a childhood dream to journey to "the land of milk and honey" the moment I arrived at the same airport. A joyful, carefree teenager, I fervently dove into my first summer in Israel. Every day brought new sights and sounds, intriguing experiences and friendships, and I imbibed them all like a sponge. I was certain I could stay there forever.

Four years later, during the course of my junior year abroad at Hebrew University of Jerusalem, I had gained the conviction that I held a place and a purpose in Israeli society. The first few months were absolutely blissful. Israel was all that I had remembered, and I was making more friends than I could count, learning more Hebrew than I could retain, and eating more falafel than I could stomach. Strangers became lifelong friends almost instantaneously, and I was eagerly welcomed into their homes. Israeli abruptness and inefficiency were amusing; bomb shelter indicators were relics of the past; and soldiers were cute in their uniforms. Every moment was full of possibility, and I reveled in the life I could create there.

My primary goals for that year were to learn Hebrew fluently, to immerse myself in Israeli culture, and to gain a deeper understanding of the dynamics of the political situation. I actively pursued ways in which to accomplish these goals, studying Hebrew fourteen hours a week at the graduate school, volunteering eight hours a week at Hadassah Hospital, spending many weekends and holidays with an Israeli family that had "adopted" me, befriending Israelis in my university dorm, and refusing to speak English in all of these scenarios. I appreciated Israeli candor and quickly understood that Israeli friendships—once gained—are unsurpassed in their sincerity and loyalty. As a political science major, I loved how politics in Israel replaced the weather in the United States as a means of making "small talk." And I strongly identified with the Israeli spirit of adventure and desire to dive into life head first. After several months, I felt I had finally broken the surface of Israeli society to find that I not only felt a deep connection to it, but that I was also unequivocally welcomed into it. I felt an overwhelming sense of belonging, and I embraced that feeling.

On the other hand, I had also engaged in enough political discussions to suspect that in the background of my carefree life in Israel there existed a marginalized and oppressed population of people about which few were divulging the true story—the Palestinians. I began to scrutinize seriously the Israeli government and its involvement in creating and maintaining these conditions, but I could not come to any conclusions without first hearing the story from the Palestinian perspective. My new mission became to understand better the reality of life for the Palestinian people and what opportunities existed to improve their situation.

I remember the night that marked a permanent alteration in my perspective on Israel. It was the fall of 1998, and I had accompanied an American-Israeli friend to a demonstration to encourage the Israeli government to implement the Oslo Accords, which called for the creation of a Palestinian state, among other steps towards "normalizing" relations between the two nations. The demonstration also coincided with President Clinton's visit to Israel. I went along to determine if this type of activism was, in fact, where my heart lay. To my astonishment, in the heat of the demonstration, as President Clinton's car was driving past us, I found myself approaching a young man holding two Palestinian flags and asking if I might hold one of them. He was taken aback at first, but eventually he handed me the flag and smiled as if pleasantly surprised. After the demonstration, he introduced himself as Farid.

Late that night, I tiptoed into my dorm room so as not to wake my roommate. As soon as I slid into bed, however, she rolled over and said, "Rachel told me you went to a pro-Palestinian rally."

"Yes," I replied, nervous about her tone and the direction of the conversation.

"Why?" she challenged, and for the first time I was asked to verbalize my recently developed convictions.

"Because I am opposed to the conditions under which the Palestinians live," I began. "And because I believe that the responsibility to ameliorate the situation rests on those with

127

power, the Israelis, as well as us, as Jews. And because—"

"But do you actually think there should be a Palestinian state?!" she interrupted, demandingly.

I took a deep breath, knowing that my response would crystallize my stance on the Israeli-Palestinian conflict and dictate my approach to the next nine months in Israel. I finally responded, "Yes."

Through numerous discussions and, in particular, by showing no hesitation in spending time in public with Farid and introducing him to my friends, I was able to gain his friendship and trust. He eventually invited me to his home in East Jerusalem to meet his family, and I slowly gained their trust, as well, and was able to visit repeatedly. Farid let me into his daily life, never disparaging Israelis or Jews, nor pitying himself or his family, but simply valuing my curiosity and the necessity for people like myself, as he would say, to be exposed to this reality. I had also befriended several other Palestinian classmates and visited them in their homes in both the West Bank and Gaza. These experiences were not only enriching and moving, but were extraordinarily enlightening.

I could no longer refer to the Palestinians as one homogenous group: they were now Farid and Wael, Fatima and Mariam—individuals with unique names and personalities. And I could not subscribe to blindly hating people who called me their "cousin," as in the Bible, and treated me as such. Nor could I brush aside the staggering disparity between the Palestinian and Israeli per capita incomes, which was evident the moment one passed through a checkpoint from Israel proper into the territories. Furthermore, I came to believe that the searching and interrogation of Palestinians at checkpoints served more as an assertion of Israeli dominance than any other practical purpose. I found this treatment to be humiliating and cruel, and it forced me to see the Palestinian resistance in a new light—in many circumstances, a normal reaction to abnormal conditions of living. My experiences demonstrated for me the urgency of implementing the Olso peace process and the responsibility I had to take action. Above all, having been exposed to both Israeli and Palestinian perspectives, I became acutely aware of the mutual lack of understanding between the two sides. These experiences filled me with purpose and inspiration to work actively to bring peace and reciprocal respect and understanding to the Israeli and Palestinian people.

By the time the spring of 1999 rolled around, I had joined several organizations and political groups, including Shalom Achshav (Peace Now), Students for Peace, Meretz and a Palestinian-Israeli dialogue group in Beit Zahor, near Bethlehem in the West Bank. It was only fitting that I joined the campaign for Ehud Barak for Prime Minister. Reported to be Yitzhak Rabin's protégé, and a firm believer in creating a life of peace and dignity for both sides, Barak's campaign slogan was, "Yesh tikvah im Barak – There is hope with Barak." I truly believed it. With an intense spirit, I spent days on end passing out pamphlets and stickers, hanging banners over highways by moonlight, and rallying in city squares. On the night the election votes were tallied, I heard the news while riding a bus back to campus. I immediately hopped off the bus and ran back to the city center to celebrate in the streets with the rest of the Barak supporters! I was full of energy and promise at that moment, and I was convinced that if all of the supporters of peace could band together, we would be invincible. I was in my element, at last, and I was certain that I could not be better suited for a life in any other place.

Only a few weeks later, the academic year had come to a close, and it was time to pack up my bags. I remember sitting alone in my dorm room, with my half-packed bags in a circle around me, shedding gallons of tears for my new home. I boarded the plane kicking and screaming from within. On the exterior, I was softly crying, and a woman sitting next to me asked in Hebrew, "What is wrong, dear?" I was so distraught that I could not find the words to answer her in Hebrew. Instead, I replied in English, "I am homesick for Israel already." She answered in perfect English, "Oh, I see. I understand. I moved here when I was about your age, and every time I have to go back to the States, I feel a little ache in my heart. But the nice part is, every time you return to Israel, you will feel that much more lucky to be here."

Now, a year and a half later, I am again leaving this place once again with tears steaming down my face, but this time I am also leaving with an intense anger in my heart. I wonder how I arrived at this moment from that one. How did I lose that tremendous passion and confidence? Was it naïve of me to believe that enough of us sincerely wanted to see a just end to the conflict? Or, perhaps, am I giving in too soon? I feel guilty for leaving and not seeing my purpose through, and yet, I know that I am incredibly unhappy and unfulfilled here. I mistrust my own perceptions of reality, and I wonder how I can love and hate a place with such equal intensity. My heart aches and my knees tremble, and I desperately long to return to a time when my love for Israel was uncompromised and I was able to reconcile that love with my belief in the profound need for change.

I fly my mind back two years to Hadassah Hospital, where, as a volunteer, I used to sit with one patient, Yoseph, for hours in the stairwell while he would chain-smoke directly beneath the "no smoking" sign, and we would sing Billy Joel and Elton John songs together. He would teach me Hebrew, and I would teach him English. And each of us would let out full belly laughs as the other would mispronounce the new words. There was nothing complicated in those interactions, nor in the inevitable moment when his Arab nurse would catch us and, with a smile and a wink, ask me to help Yoseph back to his room.

Two years later, I have returned to Israel only to succeed in immuring myself in my own Israeli-Palestinian conflict. The first few months after I had returned to Israel, two weeks after my May 2000 college graduation in Baltimore, I had been on a high. I had quickly reintegrated myself into Israeli culture and society, and I was determined to build a life there. It was an easy task at first. My Hebrew had come back almost immediately, and I had landed myself a gig as a bartender and a singer in a band. My apartment was on the roof of a building in the central market, and I could get lost for hours watching the life below me. I imagined my friends at home living lives spent searching

130

for entry-level positions and trying to make ends meet, and I could not get over how lucky I was to be living mine. By mid-summer of 2000, one could feel the tensions mounting in Israel. The peace agreements had still not been implemented, and it was only a matter of time before the progressively heated situation would come to a boil. I ignored this tension, and the subsequent violence that erupted in September, in order to convince myself that I still could create a permanent life here.

For a very brief moment, the situation was thrilling. Friends and family would call from the States, and I would play the heroine, courageously living and breathing history. My mother would call every couple of days to check in on me, complaining that she was unable to sleep at night, worrying about me. With each phone call, she would ask more firmly if I would like to come home. I laughed off the idea, claiming that the situation was not as severe as the media was reporting in the states and that, regardless, this was where I belonged. I even tried on the Israeli mentality, emulating my friends' reactions: "Bomb, what bomb? Pass the salt." However, as the violence intensified—and I withdrew into a state of constant anticipation—I could no longer maintain this act. Eventually, my fear, coupled with my ideological conflict with the Israeli stance and retaliations, took hold of me.

The day Israel invaded the West Bank, I pressed "pause" on my life. The bar was not attracting business, and the band's performances had come to a halt. The country had partially shut down, indefinitely awaiting a sign to return to normalcy, or the Israeli semblance of it. Idle, I became a slave to the news, only leaving my apartment for a place guaranteed to have a radio or a television, and to which I could reach within the fifteen minutes between each news update. Almost unthinkingly, I had begun to conduct my life in fifteen-minute segments.

Every journey outside of my apartment was frightening. I tried to avoid taking the bus as much as possible, and strategically would take buses that traveled through both Jewish and Arab neighborhoods, assuming that no one would want to harm their own people. Even so, every bus ride was potentially the last one I would survive, and though I knew it was ridiculous, my automatic response was to scan every passenger for anything "suspicious." I would skirt around any unattended package for fear that it might be a bomb, and I would avoid standing near soldiers, a known target for attacks. I was careful not to be stuck indoors for very long where I could not escape an explosion. This was a particularly difficult task, given the length of lines at any Israeli post office, bank, or health clinic. And despite my meticulous planning, I was living in the single most frequently bombed section of Jerusalem, *Shuk Mahane Yehuda* (the central open-air market). I stopped sleeping more than an hour at a time, and I ceased leaving my apartment alone after dark. Not a day went by without at least one panic attack that left me in a flood of tears.

It was as if I had gone into emotional shock. On one level, I felt truly betrayed—to the point of actual heartbreak—by my homeland. For as long as I could remember, I had put so much of my faith and love into this place, and it had turned on me. I had long understood that Israel would make political decisions of which I was not proud, and that I would know individual Israelis with whom I would never agree about politics. But I had never before doubted that Israel's intentions were pure. In the past, I could always reassure myself with the conviction that by virtue of being the Jewish homeland, Israel must uphold the Jewish values of justice, peace, tolerance, and *tikkun olam* (healing the world).

I found myself living a nightmare in which I saw a completely different side of the same country. I realized that just as Israel could welcome me as one of her own and teach me to truly live and honor this beautiful life, she could also hate, humiliate and intentionally oppress an entire population. I simply could not reconcile these two realities into one Israel: one had to be the truth, the other the lie. That the same people who had known thousands of years of persecution and strife could turn around and inflict the same pain on another people was beyond my comprehension and not only filled me with rage, but also with utter shame. I no longer felt justified in holding my Israeli passport.

My disillusionment was further intensified when it finally occurred to me that by simply signing on dotted lines over the course of a few weeks, I had obtained citizenship—the one thing that every Palestinian has coveted for longer than I have been alive—in not a first, but a second country. I saw the "law of return" that had allowed me to obtain citizenship so effortlessly, and the fact that I had subscribed to that idea, as a total affront to the Palestinian people. I began to conceive of my citizenship as having theoretically displaced a Palestinian. Furthermore, I concluded that to have sought a second citizenship, I must be inherently greedy and unappreciative of my American citizenship, and I was completely ashamed of myself. It then occurred to me that I was even more ungrateful to be thinking of the option of leaving, when few Israelis, and far fewer Palestinians, had that option. Thus, to leave was as slighting as to stay, and I felt as though I were trapped between two decisions, both of which I thoroughly rejected. Finally, it was the most profound loneliness I had ever experienced that drove me to accept my mother's offer to fly me back to the states. As much as I tried, I was no longer able to see eye-to-eye with any of my Israeli or Palestinian friends. Whether secular or religious, rich or poor, dovish or hawkish, not a soul could empathize with my current view of the conflict and the country, and I felt completely misunderstood by all sides.

I had tried to talk to my Israeli friends and convince them that the Israeli retaliations were unjustified and inhumane. I tried to convince them to view each Palestinian as an individual, instead of harboring the "us versus them" mentality that seemed so prevalent on both sides. Some agreed, but were unwilling to take action. Others dismissed my beliefs as those of a young, naïve idealist, or even worse, an American "outsider." In an attempt to "escape" the dismal mood of the country, my roommate and fellow band member and I took a weekend trip up to Tzfat, a beautiful town in the north of Israel. When he was a young teenager, he had studied there in a yeshiva, a Judaic school. He still had friends there, and they welcomed us both into their home. I was not raised in the Orthodox tradition, but I was aware of all of the strict laws surrounding Shabbat, and I had carefully planned my clothing and behavior so as not to offend anyone. This all went awry late that Friday night.

We had gathered a group, mostly men, to climb to the top of a hill to play music and drink wine together. Although it is forbidden in the tradition of many Orthodox men to hear a woman other than one's wife sing, they were happy to allow me to sing, after I had politely asked. We were all enjoying each other's company, and I was beginning to change my view of the religious in Israel as being contemptuous towards secular Jews, as well as completely ignorant to the cause of the Palestinians. At one point, I struck up an intriguing conversation with one of the men about our respective courses of study and career goals. When I began to tell him of my intention to study human rights law, possibly the following year in Israel, his demeanor shifted slightly and he seemed on edge. He asked whose human rights I was interested in defending. I told him women's, and reluctantly, Palestinians.

He immediately launched into a debate, asking, "Do you actually know any Palestinians? Do you know what they're like?"

I told him about Farid and other my friends from the university, the Palestinian women with whom I had shared a common room and kitchen in the dorms, and my friends in Gaza. He insisted that every one of them was secretly a terrorist, befriending me to eventually use me in a ploy to sabotage Israel. He said, "Don't you understand how deeply they hate us and how much they want to kill us?!"

I denied the truth of that statement, saying, "Every Palestinian is a unique individual. You cannot accurately say, 'Them!'"

He said that it was incredibly juvenile of me to think this way. I tried to counter him, but my Hebrew could not keep up with his, and soon the others had joined the debate, adding that if I were truly a Jew, I would not speak like this. Appalled, I said that my beliefs come directly from the Jewish teachings. With that statement, at least ten of the fifteen gathered rose and began to descend the hill. Only my roommate and his closest friend there accompanied me in my devastation. As we walked down the opposite side of the hill, we could still here them shouting, "She deserves to die! Any friend of an Arab is a mortal enemy of the Jews!"

The week leading up to my departure, I was watching television with some friends in Ramla, when the news broke through that two Israeli soldiers had been trapped in a Palestinian police station and brutally lynched while crowds of Palestinians cheered. I was aghast, and for the first time, I had no defense or explanation for this act. A moment later, my friend broke down in tears as they released the names of the soldiers and she realized that one was a childhood friend of hers. While it tore my heart apart to hear her call the Palestinians "animals," I remained silent. In fact, though I despised myself for it, part of me wanted to agree with her. I realized then that I was not going to convince anyone experiencing daily conflict to humanize the other side overnight. Moreover, I had run out of ways to say, "But they are human beings, too." I was physically and mentally exhausted, and I no longer believed I possessed a solution to this conflict.

I was just shy of completely giving up when I remembered Farid. Desperately trying to revive dialogue and understanding, and to distinguish myself as one of the "good guys," I called his home in the West Bank. But even my friendship with Farid had become strained, as he would talk of carrying bodies to the closest hospital and I of my mere fear of being attacked. This time Farid would not talk to me. He said, "Emily, I know you believe in peace, but right now we are not on the same side." His words burned inside me, and I felt completely helpless and defeated. It seemed that my indignation on behalf of the Palestinians was unappreciated by both sides and that, perhaps, the only people in this world who could understand my perspective were observing the conflict from their living room couches abroad. The prospect of joining them sounded relieving, and yet artificial and removed from the place to which I now felt a conflicted allegiance.

VIOLENCE IN THE HOLY LAND

For a short time I was able to sustain myself with my stubborn determination to finish what I had started and prove once and for all my independence and self-sufficiency. To leave was, to me, to render myself a failure, and the fear of living with that label caused me to reject my friends' and family's pleas for several weeks. Finally paralyzed by guilt and disillusionment, and weakened by loneliness and physical illness that had resulted from my anxiety and insomnia, I reluctantly accepted the plane ticket to Boston. I did have one stipulation, though: I would not fly home unless the ticket was round-trip. I refused to leave Israel without the option to return if I found I had made the wrong decision.

The return flight has long since expired, and though a tiny part of me still questions whether I should have left Israel when I did, I know that I was in desperate need of healing my wounds from a distance. Upon returning to the U.S., I was certain that no one could empathize with my experiences, and I felt alienated by the unconditionally pro-Israel stance of most American Jews with whom I spoke. Shortly after I moved to Brooklyn, I met a woman in a coffee house whose story from Israel twenty years ago was almost identical to mine. Through joining her organization, the Brooklyn Dialogue Project, a group of Jews and Arabs that meet regularly for dialogue, I slowly became rejuvenated. I have since found comfort in the friends I have made who have had similar experiences from which they are also still recovering. I am overcome with hope every time I see new faces joining one another to say, "Enough is enough." Moreover, my spirit and determination to devote my life to preserving human rights in the Middle East have been renewed by the activism in which I have again become involved.

I fell in love when I was fifteen years old. Not a fleeting, teenage romance kind of love, but a profound, lifelong, vulnerable love. I fell in love with Israel. And since that time, she has broken my heart so many times it is a wonder it can still beat. But perhaps just as every human being is fallible, so, too, is every nation. And just as I have come to accept my own strengths and flaws and my lifelong undertaking to constantly better myself, I must accept Israel's strengths and flaws and, likewise, spend my life working to better her. I do not pretend to have all the answers or even to know exactly how best to go about this undertaking. What I do know is that there has to be a way to reconcile what Israel is now with what I am certain—with everything I am—that she can, and must, become. And this is my Israeli-Palestinian peace process.

■ *Germana Nijim*

Germana wrote the following e-mails to her sons, Sharif and Faris.

E-MAILS FROM PALESTINE

Wednesday, 26 Mar 2003

My sons,
Here I am. No, not in Hebron. I am with Hanada, Issa, Ghassan and Dina, who has grown two feet since last year!! Yes. Crazy. I was held at the airport in Tel Aviv for hours. I was questioned in a little room by two people while four others watched and some came and went. Then I had to wait in the terminal itself, sitting on a little bench outside the small office. Groups of people,

mostly Jews, kept deplaning and breezing through security. The doors kept opening and shutting, letting cold air into the terminal. I had packed my jacket in my suitcase, and I was getting very cold. When I told this to a security woman, she said she was sorry. Finally I lost my patience and asked her to let me get my jacket from the luggage because I was shivering. Airport security passed me on from one to the other and nothing happened. So I asked what was taking so long. They said they had called in a question and were waiting for the answer. I said, ask me the question. Chances are that I know the answer and then I can get my luggage and my jacket. No response from any of them. I waited while they waited for "the answer." So I got angry and went back to the inspection room, knocked and said, "Look, I am not asking for the moon here. I just need my jacket because it is very cold in this hall. I came to this country full of good will, but right now I am just very angry because at least you should tell me what I am waiting for. What exactly is my crime???" And then two young men gave me my passport with the three-month visa and escorted me to get my luggage.
Mama

March 27, 2003

Today I went with Ghada to visit the place I told you about. It is the Arab Palestinian shopping center in El Biri. It is run by a man by the name of Sam Bahour. It is even more impressive than I thought. Huge complex with an all glass front wall. On the upper level there is a play room with a little train, merry-go-rounds and other things for the children, all indoors, where it is safer. . . Lots of space that will be for rent, to which Sam hopes to attract the best of Arab goods. The developers wanted to bring in Burger King, but they proved to be difficult to work with, and after they opened one in a Jewish settlement, the deal fell through. Then Sam Bahour thought, why should we not use what we have instead of always thinking that foreign is best? I like his thinking.

He was born in the U.S. in Ohio, but has "come back" and has a child born here. One was born in the States. He is a wonderfully positive person. He said that the Law of Return cannot be a theory, a political issue, a philosophy. It has to become a very personal issue, in which the individual Palestinian expatriate or refugee makes the decision on whether or not to come back. Sam has been here for ten years always on a three-month visa. Which means that he has to go out of the country every three months and apply for another visa. He has put in a petition for permanent residence in 1994. He is still waiting, and does not think he will ever get it. "It is a high price we pay for being here," he said. The constant harassment by the IDF, the humiliations, the lack of freedom of movement, the physical danger to his family are burdens he and his wife have decided to endure. Because the rewards are also high. Because here he feels he belongs. This is where his roots are. Where his family grew up, where he learned his values through his parents, grandparents and other relatives and friends. This is his community, he says, and he has no intention of leaving, no matter how hard Israel will make his life.

This project is the first of five in the Occupied Territories. After the first one opens in mid-May, there are four more planned: in Jerusalem, in Nablus, in Bethlehem, and yes, in Gaza. I am so touched by his strength and determination.

In fact, I am in absolute awe of the whole Palestinian population. They go on with their lives, taking in stride hardships that make me weep with sorrow and rage. They wait at checkpoints for as long as five hours at a time, and use their forced idleness to read, talk and laugh with one another, to drink tea or coffee. What surprises me is that they don't blow up! Where do they get their strength? "They" will never break us, Palestinians say. I know what they mean.

Hanada told me of an episode at the Kalandia checkpoint, where a woman soldier put a machine gun to the head of a two-year-old girl while the mother tore her hair from her head and screamed. Others around them considered attacking the woman and killing her, but while they were deciding what to do, an Israeli superior officer from the turret saw what was happening and came screaming down. He pushed the woman soldier aside, grabbed the girl and gave her to her mother. Made the mother sit down and had some water brought to her, all the while reprimanding the heartless soldier.

"Women soldiers are the worst," Hanada said. They can be absolutely vicious. Thank God this is an isolated case, but should it happen at all?

In order to get from Ramallah to Jerusalem, you have to take three taxis. Each takes you to a checkpoint beyond which it cannot go since the driver is not a resident of Jerusalem. Then you walk through the checkpoint and take another taxi to the next checkpoint. Then another short walk and another taxi. All the cars are in horrible shape either from some encounter with violence or from the huge pot holes in the streets. "We are dying a slow death here," one of the drivers said, and still he smiled and thanked me, and welcomed me to Palestine.

Palestinians give a totally new meaning to "shock and awe!" I wish more Americans would come here and see for themselves the strength and the spirit of these people who have known nothing but military occupation, humiliation, poverty and tribulation all their lives—if they are at least thirty-six years old! This may very well be the longest occupation in history.

I hope you will come to visit and I hope Faris will come back too. All Palestinians living abroad should make it their priority to come back even for a visit. So they will experience frustration and rage. So what? People here have no other choice, and they LIVE.

Your cousins here are waiting for you all. When you can. To claim your right to visit the land that gave you your father.

I am very happy and proud to be here. I love you and Faris even more now. Because you come from invincible stock. Remember that. I hug you all tight. Yes, Sharif. Life is good.

Love and kisses from us all in Jerusalem and Ramallah.
Mama

Saturday, 29 Mar 2003

Dearest,
I keep running into people I know from last year, and that makes it ever so wonderful! The cook at the YWCA hugged and kissed me, the people at the reception the same.

One of my dear friends (and you know who you are) gave me this passage before I left. It is of great comfort to me while I am here. "Do not depend on the hope of results. . . concentrate not on the results, but on the value, the rightness, the truth of the work itself." Those of us who are here HAVE to be able to operate this way, because God knows that we will see very few results during our short stay! Thank you, my Friend, for that passage! I have it always present.

Guess who was the first speaker at our conference tonight? Give up? Jeff Halper, Director of the Israeli Committee Against House Demolition.

He gave a magnificent talk that made us want to cry and scream at the same time. I cannot tell you now all that he said, but his vision is so clear, his understanding so honest, his words so true that we can only wish he will have an influence not only on the State Department people he talks to but also on the colleagues he works and lives with in Israel.

He said that the U.S. Consulate in Jerusalem gives him access to State Department people when they come here. He says they are well informed, they understand the situation and agree that a Bantustan solution for the Palestinians is NO solution at all. He maintains that Powell and even Bush understand the issues. He says it remains to be seen whether they have the will to stand up to pressure and demand that the so-called Road Map proposed by the Quartet be implemented. He says that Israel's trump card in the U.S. is a combination of Congress, the Jewish lobby and the Christian Zionists. They make a powerful combination, powerful enough to intimidate gutless politicians (my definition) whose main concern is to retain their political position and their power.

Our emotions here are always in turmoil. We are happy,

excited, angry, frustrated all at once. We stopped in front of the American Consulate tonight on our way to our hotel for a few minutes of silent vigil. We sang an Arabic peace song, in Arabic and promptly drew the attention of the Israeli guard, who called for reinforcements on his cell phone. Peace songs in Arabic sung by Americans must be a real threat to the security of Israel. . .

Rod Debs is the minister from the Cedar Falls Unitarian Universalist Society. Katrina is his daughter. The soldiers came, carrying their rifles and followed Katrina to tell her it was forbidden to take pictures in that area and made her erase one picture she had taken. Rod was a little upset at the realization that we are just a little too law-abiding sometimes, a little too compliant. Well, we learn something every day, and with experience comes the ability to talk back to soldiers and stand up to them.

Tomorrow I will try to send you our itinerary for the conference.

I have you present all the time. I thank you for supporting my "crazy" behavior. Please know that I am so very happy and grateful to be here.
Mama

Sunday, March 30, 2003

Today was a hard day.

We went to church in small groups to different churches. I went to the Catholic Church with four other people. Afterwards we were hosted for lunch by the Young Christian Workers group. They encompass a group of Christians from different denominations, and their job is to provide information to workers about their rights, and the law; to help one another keep their sanity in this very hostile and oppressive environment; to support one another and to create a sense of community and solidarity.

In the Old City of Jerusalem there are about 32,000 inhabitants. Twenty-eight thousand of them are Palestinians who have been here for generations. American and Israeli Jews sometimes offer exhorbitant sums of money to Palestinians to sell their property. Usually Palestinians resist even though they could use the money, given the economy and the level of unemployment. Somebody succumbed to temptation, however, because Sharon was able to buy a house in the Old City, from which hangs an Israeli flag and on top of which is a huge menorah.

Sigh.

On our way back from lunch, a man ran out of his shop to greet our Palestinian guide. He spoke in English and wanted to give us a report on the war in Iraq. According to him, 1000 Iraqi civilians were killed since yesterday. He faced us and looked at us one by one. "Who is the terrorist?" he wanted to know. He himself is from Iraq, as it turns out, and he predicts great calamities to befall on Americans if this war is not stopped. We said yes, he is right and we are here in solidarity and have tried everything we knew to stop the war before coming to Palestine. "You must do more!" he said. There was anger and sadness in his voice. Then he said, "I am a Bedouin, and anyone who opposed this war is welcome in my shop, and I want him to be my guest for tea or coffee."

It was then that I started to cry. The tears just came. There was no way of stopping them. Thank God I had my sun glasses. That helped a little. I have never heard anyone verbally attack Americans before. This man's rage was real and dangerous and his sadness heartbreaking. The level of frustration seems to be even higher than it was last year when checkpoints were much more intractable and curfews more pervasive. The attack on Iraq is in a way an attack on the Arab world. That is how it is perceived here. And the consequences are too horrible to contemplate.

I can't wait to get to Hebron. This conference is beginning to feel like too much of a tourist thing to me. I need to go where I will not be one of the few American tourists roaming around this unholy city. I need to be where there will be a purpose for my presence. And that is definitely Hebron.

We are supposed to spend two nights in the Galilee but I forget when we will be going. Also we have a day planned in

Ramallah. The itinerary says, meeting with the president. I have not had a chance to ask if that means Arafat. If so, do you think it would be improper to ask him why the hell he does not retire and let Palestinians get on with their lives???

I love you all, and I miss you very much especially today when my heart is full of the sadness of war.
Mama

Monday, 31 Mar 2003

My dearest sons,
Well, it seems that the fun is over. Today we went to Bethlehem and waited forty-five minutes at the checkpoint, not knowing if we could get inside the city or not. First the soldiers told us we could not pass because we had to first go and get a written permission from the commander (about one hour round trip) then finally they agreed to call him on the phone. Our seven Protestant pastors got off the bus and stood by it with their clerical collars clearly showing. We always hope that the collars will make a difference. . .

This time it must have. Because suddenly we were told, "Go!" So we left immediately. That is the protocol. When you are told go, you go.

Palestinians coming from Bethlehem and going on foot through the checkpoint can never be sure that they will be allowed to pass. If relatives have brought them there by car, they wait to see what happens. If the word is "go," they wave to one another and then take off in opposite directions, one back to Bethlehem and one to Jerusalem. How do people live never knowing what the day will bring? If they will make it to work? How late they will be, if they do make it?

We visited the university and talked to students. "We are supposed to be students, kids, " they said. "But we have no life. After 9:00 p.m. no one dares be on the street, even when there is no curfew because it is dangerous. A ten year old was killed just the other day. We are not allowed to go to Jerusalem

or any other West Bank town without a permit. Everything we
do is regulated." And yet they smiled and burst out laughing at
their English mistakes, sometimes, and had a sparkle in their
eyes, as well as a deep sadness.

But this is what I must tell you. Tomorrow morning we
are packing an overnight bag and taking off for the Galilee. We
will be gone two nights and two days. So, no messages for the
next two days.

But after I come back, how about giving me a quick call?
Just to hear your voice. Because the harder things get over here,
the more I miss you and want to put my virtual arms around
you.

Love and greetings to all. I keep you close to my heart
always.
Mama

Thursday, April 03, 2003

My dearest Sons,
Yes, I am back from the Galilee. We have had our ups and downs.
Touch and go whether or not we could enter Nablus, and
Bethlehem. But we did. Today I am very tired, and I don't know
where to start telling you what happened. Nothing bad, so don't
worry. Just a little frustrating at times not knowing whether or
not you will get to where you want to be. But then, we know
that Palestinians live like this every day.

The biggest shock was to see the electrified fence that is
being built to separate Palestinians from Israel. In more densely
populated areas, the separation wall, the apartheid wall, is going up causing a lot of grief. It is eight meters tall (that is like
four Sharifs on top on each other), and it separates families from
their relatives, farmers from their fields, people from their places
of worship. Ninety-two shops were bulldozed to prepare for
the building of the wall. We saw the rubble and could hardly
believe our eyes.

Palestinians have said to Israelis that if they wanted to

build the wall on the 1967 borders they would help the Israelis build the blasted thing, but of course, that is not how the wall is being planned. It seems that every day the plan changes to take in more land, leaving the Palestinian population more despondent and more desperate than ever.

The only good thing today was that I waved to a Palestinian shepherd across the electrified fence, and he waved back. Only God knows what must have been going through his mind, since we were at the lookout that Sharon uses to inspect the progress being made.

The Galilee was beautiful. So peaceful and so far away from the reality of the occupation.

Must go and lie down. I feel worn out and my shoulders and neck are killing me. And here I thought I was not in the least tense. . . . But the anger eats away at me, as it does with everyone else in the group.
Much love and hugs to you all.
Mama

Friday, April 04, 2003

Hello!
Today I am going to Ramallah with Sabeel. I am reminded of a conversation I had with Ghada last week.

Ghada lives in Ramallah. Her husband has a shop in Jerusalem. "Oh, things are much better now compared to last year," she said. Last year at this time there was curfew in Ramallah. The tanks were roaming the streets causing havoc. IDF soldiers were entering homes and public buildings and breaking or defacing every thing in their path.

Yes, things are better now. Her husband is able to go to work, for instance, which is a huge blessing. Of course he must take two taxis to get to work, and if he drives his car, he spends from one hour to five hours to go through the checkpoints. But he can get to work.

Things are better, calmer. IDF are not so quick to point

rifles at people. Maybe they are less afraid themselves, these young kids who look like teenagers playing at war. Only they have real rifles, and real bullets.

The checkpoint to Ramallah closes at 9 p.m. The barbed wire is stretched out across the street, and if you are still waiting to get through, that is too bad. And if you are late getting back from your work and the checkpoint closes in front of your eyes, you had better know where you will spend that night. There are no exceptions. Once the checkpoint is closed, it's closed.

Yesterday we found out why our bus was not permitted to enter Qalqiliya, in the north. Tulkarm is close to that town, and it seems that the two most recent suicide bombers were from Tulkarm. No proof of course. IDF gathered all the men from Tulkarm ages fifteen to forty. They took their IDs and their cell phones. They put them in trucks and carted them away to a refugee camp ten km. away. One thousand men, carried away like cattle. Another thousand or so were made to walk the distance since they were late reporting to the detention center. By last night the men were back home, after spending thirty-six hours of fear and uncertainty. Their families at home could do nothing but wait. Hoping that their men would come back.

Things are better now. Calmer, said Ghada. No one got shot. Thank God for that.

A few words on the Wall. Two percent of the West Bank is to be confiscated in the northern Palestine on the first phase of the wall. At some points, the wall will be six or more km. inside the Green Line. As of December 2002, some 11,500 dunums of land have been razed for the footprint of the wall, including the uprooting of 83,000 trees.

Over thirty-one groundwater wells will be in the confiscated areas of the wall's first phase. The wall will separate water sources from agricultural lands. Water pipes have been destroyed at the tune of 35,000 meters thus far. A number of villages will lose their ONLY source of water.

Things are better. Calmer. We can even try to go to Ramallah today. "Try" is the key word. We are not assured passage. Nobody has assured passage.

Love and hugs to you all.
Mama

Saturday, April 05, 2003

Hello!
The Iowa Five (Rod, Katrina, Kent, Abigail and Germana) had a good day in Ramallah today!
We had a very good lecture by Mustapha Barghouti, who had a powerpoint presentation full of facts and figures. It made our hair stand on end. Frightening what has happened to Palestine in the past two years! The litany of abuses is endless: assassinations, land confiscation, closures, curfews, beatings, imprisonments, humiliations. The numbers are staggering. Since 1967 it is estimated that 650,000 Palestinians have been detained, most of them without charge.
Barghouti told me that if I wanted to do volunteer work for the *Palestine Monitor*, I could start tomorrow. I would get a place to live in, of course, but we did not talk details. If I were not committed to CPT, I would jump at the chance.
But let me backtrack a moment. At the Qalandia checkpoint, an IDF soldier came inside the bus to check our papers. Before he left he told our group leader to tell us it was for security. Nothing personal. Then he added that he himself was from Ohio, and if there was anyone from Ohio in the bus, he wanted them to know he was saying hello. Which prompted one of my colleagues to observe: "He does not have a clue, does he?"
After Barghouti, we listened to Jean Zaru, a woman of great eloquence and intelligence. She was incredible. She said, "When we cry out it is not because we want pity. It is a way to energize ourselves, to keep the hope alive that we are still part of the international community." She went on to say that rage becomes love in the service of others.
After lunch we listened to Hanan Ashrawi, who should become, it was our consensus, the president of the new, free, independent Palestine. She is most impressive. She said that

148

when she spoke to Condoleza Rice, the woman gushed to her, "Oh, I have read all that you have written and I have listened to you so many times!" To which Hanan responded, "Then you have no excuse!" Not afraid to speak her mind, this brave, intelligent, articulate woman!

Any document, she said, is as good as its implementation, and so far none of the documents with the so-called agreements was implemented. Not Oslo, not Camp David, not Madrid, not Paris, not Sharm El Sheik. And there is little hope that the Road Map will have better success. But one must always hope, she said.

Then we visited Ein Ariq, a small village outside Ramallah, which is a model of cooperation between Muslims and Christians. There are two churches and a mosque in the village. The Muslims cook the food for Christian funerals, and Christians do the same for Muslim funerals. They help each other in cleaning the places of worship, and they live together in complete harmony. Why should we be surprised at this, though? Should not people of faith, any faith, be able to respect the beliefs of others?

Then in late afternoon we visited the Muqat, the compound that serves as prison and home for Arafat. We were shocked by the devastation. Nothing that I had seen on TV prepared me for this sight. We walked around taking pictures and swallowing hard to keep tears at bay. Then we went inside the only standing building, reconstructed since last year, where we waited a few minutes before Arafat appeared.

I will write more about the visit with Arafat later. I feel so grateful to be here. What have I done that is good in this world to deserve so much in life? Aside from having been an exemplary wife and an incomparable mother, that is??? Ha ha ha ha ha ha.

Please know that I will not be able to write as often when I am in Hebron. Probably not more than once a week. But I will try and do the best I can.
Hugs and kisses,
Mama

VIOLENCE IN THE HOLY LAND

Monday, April 07, 2003

We are back in Jerusalem for the night and tomorrow I am off to Hebron. I hope to be able to write often, but please do not expect daily messages. I will do the best I can. OK?

That's all for now. I LOVE you very much. What do you say about all of you coming to the Sabeel Solidarity Visit next year? ??? You would never regret it! It is a life changing experience.
Love,
Mama

Tuesday, April 8, 2003

Dearest Sons,
The Iowa people are on their way home, and I am in Hebron— finally! This is the way it went: we took a service (shared taxi) as far as it could go toward Hebron, about thirty-five to forty minutes. The shocks in the service were shot and sitting in the back seat virtually meant taking life in your hands. The meal I had last night threatened to find its way back. . . . but thank God all that went wrong was that the pain in my neck got considerably worse. We got off the first taxi and found young boys with carts offering to carry our luggage to the next taxi. These are home-made carts that threaten to come apart with every bump they go over. I insisted on giving the boys our business. They certainly can use the money.

We walked behind the boy over rubble and dirt mounds, and I was grateful that there was no rain to turn the dust and dirt into mud. We got into the next taxi, which again took us as far as the road permitted it to go. Then we hired another little guy who had a wheel barrow, in which he piled our stuff and that of an older woman who was coming back from a shopping trip to Jerusalem. The wheel barrow was full to overflowing, and one of the old woman's bags did not fit, so I carried it for her; she was happy. We walked behind the boy for another six or seven minutes until we reached the next *maksom*. (This is a Hebrew word meaning "checkpoint," but Palestinians use it to mean un-manned dirt mounds created by IDF soldiers in the middle of the night to block the street and prevent cars from going through. And to make life miserable for the people as well.)

I cannot tell you how angry I am to see how Palestinians have to live! Three taxis to cover a distance of thirty km! Is this living??? Climbing over man-made mounds of dirt just to prevent the passage of cars? What is it if not lunacy and harassment? And still Palestinians take it as if this were normal. This is NOT normal. This is NOT living!! I am so angry!

I need to go upstairs to my room and write in my journal. I hope tomorrow to share some impressions that have been milling around in my head.
I love you all very much.
Mama

Wednesday, April 09, 2003

I went prepared not to like him. Like everyone else, I had seen his scruffy face on TV; I had listened to his inarticulate utterances; I had criticized his choice of clothes and wished that he would look a little more western, a little more polished, a little more like "us." "I will go and see him," I said to myself, "because it is part of the Solidarity Visit, but I will NOT like him."

After wandering around the devastated compound (the Muqat), where a Palestinian flag had been planted in a trash barrel high on top of the remains of a building, I felt the impact of the ferocity of the Israeli repeated attacks on the Muqat. Those attacks were meant not only to destroy, but to humiliate, to demoralize, to break the spirit of the Palestinian authorities and of all the Palestinians watching the tanks doing their nefarious work.

We were then ushered into a large hall, newly rebuilt, where chairs had been arranged in three rows for the forty of us. We did not go through metal detectors. No one looked inside our bags or asked us to leave our cameras outside. We sat in our chairs, prepared to wait for Arafat's appearance. "I will NOT like him," I said to myself, not willing to be impressed by the lack of security.

We did not have to wait long. Arafat entered the hall with a small entourage, and if his security men were armed, we would not have known since they carried their weapons discretely out of sight. We rose to our feet and applauded because that was, after all, the expectation. Arafat IS a head of state, such as it is. A short row of chairs had been set up facing us only a few feet away. Arafat shook hands with each one of us, walking alone down every row of chairs. Then he sat across from where I was sitting, flanked by three of his ministers, who, as I learned later, are all Christians. Six or so security men stood a few moments behind Arafat, and then sat very inconspicuously on side chairs.

Arafat looked around and smiled at us. I looked hard at him. He looked small, thin, pale, sad. Our group leader introduced us as a Solidarity group, and he smiled again. "Come closer," he said. "Form a circle so I can see all of you." And we all moved our chairs closer to him.

And then he spoke. In English. Occasionally searching for the proper word, often prompted by his ministers. The words came haltingly. His tone was subdued. The man who has been "married to Palestine" for over forty years was sad, defeated, living in the betrayals and failures of the past, expressing and clinging to a hope in which he no longer seemed to believe. He had no plans or visions of Palestine to share with us. The past was clear, and dismal. The future was wrapped in a dark, ominous cloud.

I felt my heart warm to him in spite of myself. The man has been a prisoner in his own office for over a year, watching virtually all of the walls of his compound collapse around him. He works, eats, and sleeps in his office, which he shares with one of his ministers. No family life for him. No relaxed evenings with loved ones.

At the end of the audience, which had seemed more like

an informal meeting of old friends, he shook hands and posed for pictures with all who asked, without hurrying, looking at each person in the eye and smiling happily. "These are his only happy moments," I thought. And when he learned that my husband had been a Palestinian and was no longer living, his eyes filled with sadness, took my hand and kissed me twice on the top of my head. It was a sincere, spontaneous gesture that seemed to come from his heart. A few minutes earlier, he had jumped from his chair to retrieve from the floor the camera of one of the American visitors.

My heart filled with immense pity for this broken man, and my eyes filled with tears. For all his faults, real or imagined, for all his failures, here was a man who had not lost his humanity. Yes, I liked him.

Thursday, April 10, 2003

Guys,
This morning we went on our school patrol, as usual, and we were stopped at a certain point and told we could not walk on Shuhada Street. It is reserved for settlers, you see. Yesterday we had to show our IDs; today we were denied passage. So we went up another road, through the cemetery, and down the other side in order to get to the school neighborhoods and do what we needed to do. The little children smile when they see us, especially the little ones, and especially the girls, who come to us and shake our hands. It is very sweet. I said hello to two settler kids today, who only glared at me. At least they did not throw rocks.

On our way back home, we thought we would push things a bit and started walking back on the same settler road. We almost thought we had made it through, when a different soldier came up to us to stop us and tell us that that was a closed military zone and we were not allowed to be there. We said that if it was a closed military zone, then no one should have access, but the settlers do. So what gives? Of course they have no answers. The soldiers said, we are just following our commandant's orders. Yes, that rings a bell! I said to the soldier, "My feet got all wet walking in the tall grass in the cemetery." (I wear only sandals with socks.) The young man hesitated and then said, "Okay, then I will say 'go' but only today." So we went. What kind of orders do you think they had? Making things up as they go along, it seems. Anyway, I have made up my mind to talk to the soldiers as often as I can.

When we passed another group of soldiers at another checkpoint, I asked a soldier, "Is it going to be a good day?" "I hope so," he said. "No shooting!" I said. And he replied, "No, the guns are only for the bad guys." "I have yet to meet one," I said. "Me too," he replied. The system is crazy and it makes even "normal" people behave in a crazy manner.

There is a small park by the mosque, and as two little girls came across, two soldiers pointed their guns in their direction and raced by them meaning to scare both the children and my colleagues and me. (CPTers are not looked on with favor by most IDF soldiers.) But the children are used to this bizarre behavior, and unless there is actual shooting, they seem to pay not much attention. We just kept walking, and the soldiers got together and laughed. Is this sane???
LOVE you.
Mama

Friday, April 11, 2003

Last year when I was here I was totally unable to speak to Israeli soldiers. Much as I wanted to see them as real human beings, the arrogance of many of them, their machine guns usually held at chest level, ready to be put into action, made it impossible for me to see them as real human beings. I am not proud of that, because as a peacemaker, I ought to be able to see everyone as my brother or sister. But we all know that there are delinquent brothers and sisters . . . and IDF soldiers intent on maintaining the occupation, fit into that category for me.

One of my friends said she would pray for my anger, because that is what I felt I needed most help with. It must be working. This year I try to engage IDF soldiers in conversation and try to listen to what they have to say.

Today one of them told me he hopes for peace. He does not want to be here, he said. He wants to go back home and have a regular life. I did not suggest that he join the Refuseniks, but the next time I see him, I will. When I attended the Women in Black demonstration last Friday, the Israelis invited us to attend a rally in support of the Refuseniks, but it was to be in Tel Aviv, and unfortunately our schedule did not permit us to go. But it is good to know that apparently the number of Israelis who refuse to serve in the Occupied Territories is increasing. This is a sign of hope.

Another IDF soldier shouted at me from his camouflaged guard post that he wanted a red cap like mine. "Fine," I said, "come and join CPT." "But I am not a Christian," he said. "Then there is a problem, isn't there?" I said, "because these caps are only for CPT." He smiled from his tall post and waved, wishing me a good day.

Today a graduate of University of Northern Iowa, Mohammed Jalal, came to see me. He was in Cedar Falls six years ago, as a young man. He is still a young man, of course, only now he has a wife and three children. We decided to go for a walk through the deserted streets of the Old City, where I live. We hoped to find the gate that leads to the Ibrahim Mosque open so we could go visit together, but of course, today being Friday, the gate was closed. The road that leads to it from outside the Old City is a "settler" road, and Palestinians are not allowed on it, so whereas today I could have gone, my former student could not go.

This is a road paid for with OUR tax money, people! We tried another way and were stopped by soldiers. They looked at Mohammed's ID and then called in (God knows where) to check on him. He had no record, and I insisted that Mohammed be allowed to walk with me. The two young soldiers manning the post said they would have to call a higher up for permission.

"Okay," I said. "We'll wait." Pretty soon six IDF soldiers showed up and talked among themselves. The one with more authority apparently said no, but he would not talk to me. He would not even look at me. I had a hard time seeing him as my brother. He talked only to the two young soldiers, who felt really chagrined at having to tell us NO, no Palestinians allowed in the Jewish area. "Excuse me," Mohammed said, "it is not a Jewish area. It is Occupied Territory." The soldiers did not argue with that. They kept their guns pointing at the ground. They apologized and smiled sheepishly to show us we were truly sorry. "I am sorry too," I said, "but I am also very angry, because that road was built with American money, and the agreement was that it was going to be built to benefit both Jews and Palestinians, and now Palestinians are not allowed to walk on it? How is this helping bring peace to this area?" "I am sorry," one of the soldiers said, and he shook his head and walked back to his post. So I will continue to engage IDF soldiers in conversation whenever I can, while my blood is boiling inside me at the great injustice.

Yesterday we had decided to go and post some huge banners on the dirt barriers set up by Israel to impede traffic. The banners said in English, Hebrew and Arabic: THIS IS RACISM. As we passed through the center of town, we noticed a great crowd of men gathered together at the top of a hill. "Come, come," some Palestinians said to us. They all know CPT, of course, and we are easily recognizable by our red caps. They wanted us to join the crowd on the hill because they had just been made to close all their shops since an Israeli commander was to pass through. We consulted quickly with each other and decided that it was appropriate and necessary to join them. We unfolded our banners, and kids volunteered to hold them up for us. So we let them, while we held up the bigger ones. Things got tense. More soldiers arrived, and I had visions of tear gas being shot at us. But thank God nothing like that happened. After about forty minutes, another Jeep arrived and a soldier talked to one of the Palestinian men. The soldier told him in essence that the men could reopen their shops, "But that is not because they [CPT] are here," he said. "We are the ones who tell you you can open the shops. They did not do anything for you." Amidst great cheering, shops were reopened, and the clatter of metal shutters echoed throughout the town. We congratulated the shopkeepers as we walked along, and they said, "Thank you. Thank you. You have done a great thing for us." At least they knew they were not alone in their struggle, in their protest. And even if they did not sell a single item all day, their right to attempt to make an honest living was recognized and restored. Never mind the reason. We were happy for them. That's life in Hebron.

I LOVE you all very much. Thank you for not worrying. I am very happy here.
Love,
Mama

Saturday, April 12, 2003

I am in Jerusalem. I hope to participate in the Palm Sunday procession tomorrow and then we will go back to our very own private little hell. And Hebron is as close to hell as I ever want to be.

There are a zillion soldiers patrolling the streets these days. Sometimes they tell us we cannot pass, then after a few minutes they tell us we can go. This morning during school patrol, we saw two soldiers gathering rocks. "What are you doing?" we asked. "Practicing," they said. As we moved on, they started hurling rocks toward a guard post. And the soldiers there were laughing and chatting with each other. I ask: what the hell is this all about? Is it not an incitement? What is to be learned or gained from this exercise? And what about soldiers sneaking around corners with their guns pointed, just like they have seen done in movies? Six soldiers hugging the walls, peeking around corners, pointing guns and moving on.

The thing is that Hebron Old City is a ghost town. Very few people are ever on the streets. All the shops are closed in the Old City, except for a few little holes in the wall where an old man is selling a few miserable goods, his shelves virtually empty. Yesterday, six soldiers stood outside the tiny little mosque by our apartment, standing by the door as if they had a right to be there. Much as I try to manage my anger, it keeps resurfacing, and I am not alone feeling this way.

And yet people do laugh, and hug their children, and are proud to show them off when we admire them. The little ones run to us with a huge grin and shake our hands. In answer to our questions, they are always fine! Last night we were hosted to dinner by Temporary International Presence in Hebron. We are beggars compared to them. They have uniforms, and cars, and a bar (don't laugh—I never thought I could get a glass of wine in Hebron!!!) and there are sixty-two of them, from six European countries. Twelve of them are Italian, so I had a nice chat last night with Giuseppe, Ugo and Massimo. Don't ask for last names. It was a great evening, with really good food.

I LOVE you always and keep you close to my heart.
Mama

Sunday, April 13, 2003

Now we have a few minutes of free time, so I thought I would take advantage and tell you about this blessed Palm Sunday. In a little while we are going to go the the top of the Mount of Olives to join a procession. The rains have stopped here. Winter is over. Trees and flowers are blooming, but not with the same abundance as the garbage. The East Bank residents pay taxes to Israel, but the money does not go toward services in their areas. It goes to keep Israel, West Jerusalem, beautiful. But you know all of this already. It is just hard to take when one sees the injustice with one's own eyes.

People, PLEASE, call your congressmen and senators and write letters to the editors about the International Observers who are being killed by Israel in the Occupied Territories. They seem to be dropping life flies these days, and who is making Israel accountable for these crimes? All of us who are here on peace missions feel very much vulnerable at this time. PLEASE demand that a UN peacekeeping force be brought to the Occupied Territories. I KNOW that Israel has never agreed to have it here, but should that stop the UN from insisting on coming? And should not ALL members (well, ok, as many as possible) insist that Israel respect UN resolutions or be attacked by the "coalition" now that the bombing has stopped in Iraq?? There is an urgent, critical need for UN peacekeepers in this area. Israel is getting away with murder on a daily basis. Palestinians die a violent death at the rate of three per day. Is this acceptable? Is this not terrorism?

I LOVE you all very much. Please work for us on the front line, and for the Palestinians whose human rights are violated with impunity every single day, with the help of our tax money.

I hug you tight, and keep you close to my heart. I am happy. Really! As happy as one can be in hell.
Love,
Mama

■ *Mae Ramadan*

Mae Ramadan's family is originally from Jerusalem Palestine, but Mae was born in the United States. She is eighteen years old and a freshman at Essex County College, where she is majoring in political science and on the staff of the school newspaper. Mae has been very active in the Palestinian issue, and has written for several chronicles and newspapers. She is very proud of her heritage and the fact that she is a Palestinian American Muslim.

PALESTINIAN AMERICAN MUSLIM

I live in New Jersey where I go to a public school and am the only Palestinian American Muslim. After the horrible terror attacks on September 11th, I experienced stereotyping and discrimination directed towards my family and me. I always ignored it, although on that day, the 11th of September, I realized just how much hate can be aimed at people. I was sitting in my class when we heard that a low flying airplane hit the first tower of the World Trade Center. We all thought it was an accident. The class ended and we were on our way to our next class. My friends and I walked outside the classroom into the hallway. The hallway was very quiet, too quiet.

Suddenly the loud speaker went on and our principal told us what happened. I, along with my friends, was horrified. I was scared and did not know what to do to help my friends, most of whose parents worked in New York. Then I realized that my uncles were near New York too. So at that moment I was even more terrified to think that, God forbid, something had happened to them.

I went and called my mother; she told me that they were fine. So I went back to the library with my friends to see if they had any news from their parents. Some people were on the internet, saying that the Palestinians did it. The whole school knows that I am the only Palestinian in my school. I have written various articles in the high school newspaper and am very involved with everything to do with our culture or religion.

Students came up to me, telling me that this is my peoples' fault and to go back to where I came from. I ignored them. I knew that emotions were high and people were saying things without thinking. My friends stood by me and defended me. Later I was walking to my locker and people were yelling "terrorist" and other words at me that I had rather not say. They spat at me and threatened me. I told my uncle, who was the

160

New Jersey Councilman for the Palestinian American Congress, New Jersey chapter. He took it to a higher level. Unfortunately the principal and the board of education failed to do anything. After that incident, I wrote an article called, "Muslims are being Stereotyped," which tried to teach people the true meaning of Islam, not what is portrayed on T.V. I tried to explain what the Palestinians are really fighting for, that we are not terrorists but freedom fighters. I got my point across several times through my writing.

My school holds Unity Week every year and every year I participate. This year more than ever, I was determined to show everyone what my country and religion are really about. Every year I did Palestine. Each person involved has a wall to decorate. I made a poster with photos of the Palestinian flag, Jerusalem, a white dove, the Dome of the Rock and Al-Aqsa, various mosques, and, of course, Yasser Arafat. I put him up as a symbol of the Palestinian people; I did not put him up to start something.

This year Unity Week was in April and around that time it was very heated back home. That was when the Israelis had Arafat in confinement. People took my poster the wrong way. They made a petition and I was called down to the principal's office and was forced to take it down. I refused to do so unless they gave me a valid reason. I had to call my mom and uncles. They came down to talk to the principal but it was no use; after an hour of talking to him I had to take it down. I decided to let it go and to continue with Unity Week.

The last day of Unity Week was a culture celebration in the cafeteria. I brought in Palestinian coffee, candy, music, and put up the Palestinian and American flags to show that I love both Palestine and America. Many people, mostly the Jews, did not come to my table and ignored me. There were those who were not racist and came to my table and ate the food and wanted me to teach them to speak Arabic and to dance Arabic. So I did, and that day we brought so many different cultures together.

In June, the last month of the school year, I had a very bad experience with a racist teacher. I am a good student; I always receive an A or a B. After September 11th, he acted weird towards me. All of a sudden, my papers mysteriously got lost, my tests got lost, and my projects got lost. Mind you, I had all my grades with me. At the end of the last marking period I went up to him and asked him what my final grade was and he told me, "D." I was so mad I basically told him that he was a liar and was doing this on purpose. He did not deny it. I showed him the grades that I had. He said they were inaccurate and that I was making them up. I informed my mother; she called the school and set up a meeting with him and his supervisor. We went down to the school and we were talking to him when he told us that he had to go. My mom commented that it was not right that he was always leaving his students' problems aside. He stood up and slammed his fists onto the table and yelled at us, "If your kind of people don't appreciate what I do for my country, then leave." My mom and I could not believe what he said; he ran out of the room. His supervisor was telling us how sorry she was. My mom wanted an apology from the teacher himself. So we went down to the principal's office and there was my teacher. The principal came out and said to us, "There is nothing to talk about." My mother tried to tell him that there was more to talk about, but before she had a chance, he put his hand up in her face and told her, "This discussion is over," and closed the door in her face. So the result was he gave me the D.

I never thought that I would get so much discrimination just because I am a Palestinian Muslim. I am proud of it, but I am also an American. I heard stories from back home that my people are beaten daily and discriminated against. I thought I would not experience discrimination because I live in America. I would expect this back in Palestine, but not in America where we all are treated equally and have so many cultures, religions, and ethnic groups. Hate is a cancer that must be stopped. If it is not stopped, it will grow bigger and bigger until there is no escaping it. We are all children of God. God put us on this earth not to fight but to live and let live. To live in peace and be happy. God bless Palestine, God bless America and God bless us all.

Coffee with Ben

■ *Gahl Pratt*

Gahl Pratt, the third of five children, is a thirteen-year-old student. She left Israel with her parents at age nine. She is interested in art, politics, and peace.

COFFEE WITH BEN

"Is your brother okay?" the teachers huddled around me in my American school would ask.

"He is on the front lines over in Israel, you know," they would add to the nearest impressionable colleague.

In class, a boy asked me, "So, who's winning?" I pretended not to hear, but the boy pressed on. Seeing I had no way out of it, I replied, "The gravediggers."

After allowing himself to swallow that, he added, as an afterthought, "Your brother, what kind of gun does he have?"

"The kind that shoots," I replied, "the kind with a trigger, the kind that goes 'boom.'"

Later, standing in the gym on wooden floors in my squeaky sneakers, I shot from the foul line. Swish, swish, swish. The ball glided into the net twelve times before finally bouncing off the rim and landing on the floor. Boom. In Israel, it never used to go "boom," because my brother and I practiced our foul shots on sandy earth. When it hit the ground, there was no sound of rubber on wood.

My brother Ben used to say that his head was a basketball with a face painted on it. I never understood why he loved the game so much. He got really excited when my American grandparents brought him a pair of squeaky basketball shoes from New York. In kibbutz Revivim in the Negev desert where we grew up, there were no wooden courts to squeak them on; we used to play barefoot. To add to my bewilderment at his devotion to the sport, there were the coaches. They could argue for hours about a foul shot or a double dribble, they could train their teams not only to play, but also to conspiracize against

163

anyone else in the league, but even after all that, the players didn't much care. All they wanted to do was live their life, and their life was basketball. Perhaps it's like the government, manipulating its people and brainwashing their armies into that idea, whatever it might be, until they are ready to blindly serve Sharon, Arafat, Big Brother, God; but then again, I don't understand much of that, either.

Ben doesn't shoot baskets anymore. I choose not to think of what he does shoot. When he had leave and we visited him at home on the kibbutz, in his tiny graffiti-infested room, my brother and I sat alone, sipping hot mugs. I was not allowed to drink coffee, but Ben made me some anyway, and I was busy shoveling in one spoonful after another of sugar.

"Don't do that," he said, "sugar only makes it sweeter, but it blocks out the special bitterness of coffee. It makes it lose the true flavor."

This was not the first time I'd heard this. Upon visiting the tent of our Bedouin friends, we drank with them their coffee, which was black, harsh and bitter. Their tradition said that it symbolized life. After finishing a big cup of the fragrant drink, following the rules of hospitality, we were served a tiny glass filled with the sweetest tea one could imagine. The tea, they made it known, symbolized hope.

When someone asked my mother how she feels about her son using a gun, she answered defensively, "The only thing my son shoots is a syringe. He is a medic." I had not known this before hearing that, but the idea made me laugh. First we shoot them with bullets, then with syringes.

We have no emotional problems when talking to Ben on the phone. Recent subjects include his new girlfriend, our cousin's dancing career, and, yes, basketball. He never calls from the base, always from home, from his room on Sabbath leave. I've never heard an army story from him. My brother Ben has been in the army for two years, but I have never seen him in uniform.

Sometimes we like to pour a whole lot of sugar in our coffee.

Hope

■ *Shira Rubin*

Shira Rubin is fourteen years old and was born in the United States; her mother and relatives are Israeli. Shira has made annual trips to Israel throghout her life and is deeply concerned with conflicts in the Middle East and the prospect for peace in the region.

HOPE

Beginning to face the issues of the world, I, an unsure, naive girl gained much wisdom from a friend I would least expect it from. This friend taught me about some of the most important things in life. I met Selima during sixth grade, as an off-beat eleven year old, taciturn and without many friends. She had an olive tone to her skin and dark, thick hair. At first I figured her to be Israeli. She moved to my town, a middle class New Jersey sub-urban community, about a month before.

Our English teacher had partnered Selima and I together for a project on our family trees. The assignment was to design a family tree and write descriptive stories about the history and members of the family. Then we were to read it to our partner. As I dragged my desk over to her, producing a vexing screech, I was a little apprehensive about working with Selima, for I sel-dom, if ever, had spoken a syllable to her before.

I took the liberty of explaining my anecdotes first.

"My mother moved here from Israel," I started.

As soon as I said the word Israel I recognized a look of pain and stress on her face. After reciting my composition I asked, "Okay, I'm finished, now can you tell me about your family Selima?"

In a low voice she began, "My parents and I are Palestin-ians. We moved here from the West Bank."

I began to comprehend the earlier discomfort. With mel-ancholy she explained, "Almost my entire family are members of the PLO and its branches."

I was absolutely appalled and a million questions ran

through my mind at once. "What kind of girl is this? Who is she? Does she hate Jews?" But my thoughts disappeared when she filled me in on the reason why her family moved to the U.S. They were absolutely revolted by the actions of their family. Selima's mother and father were peace lovers who only wished for co-existence. They had traveled to America to get away from the region's chaos. Although Selima was hopeful for peace ever since she was born, when she arrived in the United States, she began to put herself in the shoes of Israelis more frequently. Respectful of each other's feelings, we poured our views out to each other.

"Palestinian children, like Israeli, long for the ability to go outside and play with their friends and not have fear cross their minds," said Selima.

"I know," I said, "it is absolutely tragic. Girls and boys of five years should not have to think such disturbing thoughts. Worry and fear should not have to be characteristics of children."

"But you have to understand; my relatives are good people at heart."

"I understand, Selima."

That was maybe one of the most profound conversations I had ever had. We resolved that the only way that peace can be achieved, is to make a complete, honest agreement. For forty-four minutes (the length of the class) Selima and I discussed the Israeli-Palestinian conflict. And together we gained Israeli-Palestinian hope and established a sacred bond.

Selima and I received a zero for English that day because we did not present our projects. But we obtained so much. By simply learning about Selima's life, I realized that peace is possible. By merely teaching tolerance, Israelis and Palestinians can live side by side. Selima had learned to see the perspective of Israelis, and I took a walk in her shoes, which provided us both with hope. The only path to harmony is looking through your opponent's eyes. Together, Selima and I wished for peace. Because peace will only happen with time, we prayed that our wish would become a reality one day. Selima moved three months after that project and I never heard from her again.

EPILOGUE

■ *Marcia Kannry*

Marcia Kannry, a Jewish American, lived in Jerusalem for several years. She was a Jewish community professional until the first Intifadah. In September 2000 she founded The Dialogue Project, a non-profit which gathers Palestinians, Jews, Arabs (Muslim and Christian), non-Arab Muslims and all supportive others, into monthly dialogue circles around New York City and the Northeast. You can contact her and learn more at www.thedialogueproject.org.

CREATING DIALOGUE: HEARING THE OTHER

I lay in bed on the morning of September 16, 2000 and I heard the news about Ariel Sharon walking on the Temple Mount. That morning I knew immediately that the walk was a provocative act and that the Barak government had made a mistake. I wanted to find someone who would be as concerned as I and perhaps we would talk about this. I was not yet thinking of dialogue. There was some connection with Palestinians here but I didn't know what.

When I went to synagogue—that was after a week of violent clashes in which mostly Palestinians had been killed—all I heard was everyone talking about "they this, they that." Meanwhile the news reports were about Palestinian and Jewish deaths, but at the synagogue it was all about "they." I had never told anyone at the synagogue my personal story and something that day happened and I began talking to people about my prior life in Israel. It was just my need to shock them into what I thought was tragedy, a human tragedy. I would say, "Who is 'they'? Who do you mean when you say 'they'?" And somebody would respond, "The Arabs," and I would ask them to be more specific. I would say, "I don't know who the Arabs are any more than I know who the Jews are." The answer kept making my soul heavy. I needed to speak of my own experience in Israel and to speak with Palestinians directly.

VIOLENCE IN THE HOLY LAND

My experience in brief: a young eighteen year old hops on a plane and lands at a kibbutz in 1971. She is spiritual, hearty and horny. A potent combination to bring to the Israel of 1971, an Israel where the idea of the settlements and continued occupation was thought of as a moral and ethical wrong by the majority. The few settlers of the *Gush Etzion* (the area between Jerusalem and Hebron, annexed in 1967) were eccentrics. I fell in love, returned to the United States after surviving the requisite broken heart and yearned for Israel. I now believe I yearned for a life there which was not yet commercialized, globalized or Americanized. Most Israelis then did not have a car, unless provided by work. TV had only come to the country in 1967 and there was one channel.

Finally a few years later I made *aliyah*: I emigrated to Israel. (*Aliyah* is Hebrew for "ascent." When you leave Israel you make *yerida*, a descent.) And again fell in love—a few times. I met someone who had escaped the brutal Rumanian regime. We thought we would get married, settle down. Establish a life. He needed to complete six months of army service to fulfill his commitment to the state. On the last day, as he was hitchhiking home, standing at an army bus stop, a truck was driven into the stop, killing several, wounding many. He died. I became numb, not angry. I found a job, fell in love again, and became aware of the government and it's policies, slowly feeling the crassness, the brutality. I witnessed scenes of degradation. For example: young boys—Israeli soldiers—tell older Arab men at a checkpoint to look through a pile of shoes for their sandals. (Sandals they had been told to take off as part of a security measure). Meanwhile, a soldier had pissed on that pile of shoes.

Somehow my numbness faded and my anger surfaced. I left the country and came back to the States and began working for a major Zionist organization, bringing "missions" of American donors to Israel. And then 1987 came and Yitzchak Rabin, then Defense Minister, directed rubber bullets, house demolitions and live ammunition at student protesters and their mothers. And yes, I went and I had stones thrown at me too. But I did not need to shoot to get a Palestinian to speak with me. I just needed to ask someone, "Would you have some tea with me?" And that is when dialogue was born in my heart.

So back at my synagogue in the autumn of 2000 I kept asking people, "Have you ever spoken to a Palestinian about these issues?" And people would look at me like I was crazy. And I would say to them, "That little coffee shop where everyone sneaks out to get coffee during services, that's run by Palestinians."

That's basically the beginning of The Dialogue Project because from that moment on I began speaking directly to Palestinians and Arabs whenever I saw someone who could possibly be an Arab, a Palestinian. Stores, restaurants, law firms. I just asked. "Where are you from? Oh, is your family surviving this situation?" And people would say, "Yes, thank you for asking." And I'm sure they were thinking, "Who is this woman with a Jewish star? Why is she speaking to me?"

I went to local churches, speaking to them about getting a group together to start a dialogue. A couple of people at my synagogue were interested but afraid, really afraid. It took four months of planting seeds and strategizing first to get the social action committee at the synagogue to work with me on this project, and later the board of the synagogue, because at first they didn't want to do it.

I went to local representatives and state senators and local businesses to cover the costs of an event. We picked up eight hundred dollars. One or two of the other synagogues had one or two members that were interested. The rest, they didn't want to hear of it. "Israel's under attack, we don't want to hear of it."

A month later, there was a gathering of over 150 Jews, Palestinians and Christians in a conservative synagogue. They came to hear a Palestinian-American and a Jewish-American, both sons of refugees: one the son of a refugee of the Holocaust, another the son of a refugee of Dijan, a village the Jews paved over. That was the gathering I organized. At the end of that evening there were sixty-five people who expressed interest in dialogue.

We began meeting regularly, in small groups. It was and

is very difficult. When very grass roots people—not academics or politicians—are falling prey to the rumors and conspiracy theories of their own communities, they find it harder to come to the meetings. Because there is so much despair. The Palestinians are trying to get basic things like medical supplies and food to their families. The Jews are in pain over the suicide bombings and the anti-Judaism around the world. They come in great numbers, but they come to interrogate the Palestinians, sometimes. This makes it even more difficult for the Palestinians to come. And when they do come what we hear are pain, grief and the story of the victim told again and again.

So what we do in the dialogue groups is not to focus on grilling one another, but on actively listening, hearing the other person, putting the other person's words in our mouths. When someone tells their story, we ask people to speak what they just heard, not to reflect their opinion. And that's really hard.

As from my perspective with the brutalization of each culture—the horrific policies of the Sharon government, the beating of the Palestinians trying to harvest, the escalating violence on the Palestinian side—it's becoming more and more difficult here, in the U.S., for people who share democracy and freedom of movement, to meet. We're finding our meetings very surreal.

I keep repeating my story to the dialoguers. I keep telling them this is not the first time despair has hit a people, our peoples. Then I tell them my story. I may ask, "Why don't I go party all night because there is nothing I can do? Why don't I resort to violence because I had to identify his body?" The only choice you have as a human being is not to accept that brutality into your soul, not to accept that despair because then the enemies of human rights win. It doesn't matter if it is the enemies of Israel or the enemies of the Palestinians. Those people—the enemies of human rights—win when we let this despair polarize us. This is how the dialogue keeps going.

The Palestinians are beginning to feel the deep Jewish fear; at first they did not understand what 2,400 years of diaspora has done to the Jewish soul. I explain the Israeli-Palestinian situation with the image of a young man or woman with a strong body, looking over her shoulder while her foot is raised above another person, saying, "You killed me, you killed me." Meanwhile the person on the ground is saying, "I will make you a victim." And the standing Jew keeps saying, "Tell me I'm a victim."

We Jews have this image of a beautiful, strong Jew. That's how I came to envision the modern Jew: as a young Israeli with a rifle slung over his or her shoulder. When I was a young woman and went to live on a kibbutz, I spent my first morning picking grapefruit. I thought, "How wonderful to be with Jews." When you're young you have all that energy pouring into your body with everything feeling so right. I remember thinking, "How great that I, a Jew, am here; no one ever again will displace me." At that time I did not know that that kibbutz was built over the remains of a Palestinian village.

Later on, when I immigrated to Israel, I remember a letter I wrote my mother. I wrote that I loved being a majority culture in my own land and that this was a healthy, strong people, a little aggressive but really a healthy, strong people and that this was what the new Jews were. A brave new world. I believed all of it, with almost a physical feeling in my body. And when you're young, this is how your beliefs become enmeshed with who you are.

And then in 1980 my loved one was killed, he who I hoped to marry. Things began to change. I actually began to question the system he served. So my vision of this healthy Israel changed as my eye became opened to the occupation and I began to understand how someone could have so much rage that they could drive a truck into a group of Israeli soldiers. I needed to know more fully why there was such rage. It wasn't enough to say, "Oh, those were the Arabs."

And that's when the vision began to develop. So then I just didn't have a vision of a strong Israeli with a rifle slung causally over his or her arm. I saw this person young, strong, looking over his shoulder at 2,400 years of history saying, "Don't kill me again. You cannot kill me again. Please don't kill me any more." Kind of both thoughts.

But the rest of that image—the Palestinian under the Is-raeli foot—wasn't there yet, that happened later as I began to study Middle Eastern history, not just my people's version of the creation of the state, but the Palestinians' version, and their history. I did that in the United States. I had to remove myself to see the occupation in a clear way. And that's when the vision began to complete itself. But it became fully clarified when I returned to Israel and hitchhiked into the Occupied Territories. The news stories were so horrible: the rubber bullets, the bull dozing. I needed to see it and understand it, and that's when the occupation came into full vision for me. And that's when I finished this vision. The Jew with his foot raised saying, "You can't kill me, don't kill me" and "Tell me I'm the victim," with now a person looking up from the ground, saying, "I'm the vic-tim." That vision was completed in 1987. I realized that the Pal-estinian has the same vision. And I have no answer to it.

The occupation is over thirty years old. There is no ac-knowledgment by the Jews of the pre-1948 years when there was a population transfer. At the same time I don't hear Pales-tinians acknowledging the Jewish right to live freely, and I think that's because we took an indigenous people's land. If I lived at that time I might have done that too. We are a state under inter-national law and they are a people under international law who need a state.

I believe the most radical violent forces operating among Jews and Palestinians could lose their control and power if the Jews would acknowledge Palestinian victimization and the Pal-estinians would acknowledge the Jewish need for safety.

I feel the whole Israeli and Palestinian leadership need to be in a dialogue. Many of the activists refuse to come into dialogue because they feel they have too much work to do. It is a lot of hard work. People sometimes don't even know what they're saying. That's why in the dialogue a part is reflecting back, because through an encounter you can open a place for them to harangue, but you need to change yourself first.

There are days after dialogue I am filled with joy and there are days when I walk away with all the contradictions, the opposites, that are true for each person.

We're not looking to change the world through dialogue, but ourselves. In dialogue we ask three questions. First we ask, "What does Home mean to you? Is it a place? An idea?" Then we ask, "What is your connection to the land, physically and spiritually? And what are your family's ties to that land?" Finally we ask, "What is your attitude about the Other? How did you first hear about the Other? What did Arabs say about Jews? What did Jews say about Arabs? And what were the negative and positive views you have of the Other?"

I did this recently at the UN with Armenians and Turks, whites and blacks, and when we did this "home" exercise, the woman I did this with said, "Marcia, she is not at home in Israel, she is not at home in the United States. She does feel at home in Brooklyn." But she said, "What I hear is: Marcia's home is in dialogue." That was wonderful. That is one of those safe places where you feel warm. You can say what is scary too. And that is part of what Home is about: it's about living in the middle of something where you can explore and discover and you are safe to say what you think and feel. So dialogue is home for me.